TIMES OF RESTORATION

Orville Swindoll

Destiny Image
PUBLISHERS, MEDIA ENGINEERING
R. D. 2, Box 103
Shippensburg, PA 17257

Copyright 1983
Destiny Image
R. D. 2, Box 103
Shippensburg, PA 17257

Permission is freely granted to photocopy or generate on transparancy any portion of this book for study and review purposes. Resale or reprinting is not permitted without consent of the publisher.

Cover: Tresa Bowman   ISBN 0-914903-00-4

To my beloved fellow-workers and pastors in the city of Buenos Aires, is dedicated this story of our experiences together.

*Repent therefore and return,
that your sins may be wiped away,
in order that times of refreshing may come
from the presence of the Lord;
and that He may send Jesus,
the Christ appointed for you,
whom heaven must receive
until the period of restoration of all things
about which God spoke
by the mouth of His holy prophets
from ancient time.*

The Acts of the Apostles 3:19-21

TABLE OF CONTENTS

TIMES OF RESTORATION

	Preface	9
1	Why Contain It?	11
2	Fire On a Dry Prairie	15
3	Bound Together by the Spirit	21
4	Floodwaters	31
5	Trumpet Sound	39
6	Ready to Obey	47
7	Crowded Halls and Anointed Messengers	55
8	Tortuguitas and Nehemiah	61
9	From Revival to Normalcy	71
10	Tightening the Joints	79
11	Run with the Vision	89
12	Maturing Through Conflicts	99
13	Groundwork for Unity	109
14	Building with the Word	119
15	A Door, a Goal and a Way	129
16	Difficulties and Definitions	137
17	Concentrating On Our Homework	145
18	Mergers in the Metropolis	157
19	A Moral Framework	165
20	Growing Room	173
21	Epilogue: Our Vision and Faith	185

FOREWORD

There is a **power** in an honest testimony. I mean, a special kind of power that reverberates from the words and from between the lines as you read this account of one of God's visits to His people in Argentina.

My personal involvement in Argentina since 1963 enables me to know the events, the story and especially the men in a very real way. The honesty of the account is one of the particular strengths of this manuscript and, I believe, will be one of the reasons God can and will use it to speak to all of us who also hunger for a time of restoration!

Permit me to use the word visitation, rather than revival, for God doesn't actually **send** revival — He literally comes Himself! In the power of the Holy Spirit and in the eternal councils of His own sovereignty, He decides and He comes.

Contrary to the average Christian mind set, His coming is not always all peace and tranquility. Rather, church history records His coming as tumultuous, glorious and a mixed blessing! Mixed with accusation, misunderstanding and a Power and Presence that makes it all to be more than we can explain or comprehend.

From start to finish, Orville gives us selected "kingdom pearls" chosen out of a thousand things that could be recorded in order to grant us spiritual **insight** into the ways of God when He comes to visit.

This is above all a **Church** book. It relates everything to the strength, life, love and unity of the Church. It causes us to love the Church more with all of her shortcomings. We are forced to see that it is the Church which Christ is building, and it must find its proper place in renewal theology.

There are clear and codified kingdom

principles everywhere. Woven into the story is the redefinition and renewal of the demands of the Kingdom which always happens when God comes to visit a man, a people, or a country as He did to the church in Argentina.

The message challenges every believer to expect and to move toward the **kind** of community, participation and maturity that is described in the pages of the New Testament. The **pattern** for that search is reviewed and restored as the Holy Spirit leads, blesses and directs a people toward His grace.

The chapter entitled, From Revival to Normalcy, in my opinion, is a most important chapter. It is the apex of the story and perhaps nothing Orville has written could be more helpful. There have been visitations of God so powerful that it did not seem to matter whether there were leaders or not. God came, sovereignly and spontaneously, blessing all in His Path. The blessable and the not-so-blessable. He dealt swiftly with those who hindered His purpose.

The important aspect for every visitation, revival or renewal movement is that we learn the lesson so ably stated here by Orville: "God never allows His glory to remain at the same intensity as at the beginning of the visitation." The reason, as we learn from the following chapters, is that we are always required by the Lord to learn to **walk by faith!**

Finally, the summary lesson that comes through in a clear and prophetic tone is that God's Way will work under all circumstances, not only during those times when His Glory is so evidently manifest.

This book, read with an open heart and spiritual understanding, will reward the reader with his own "time of restoration"!

Bob Mumford

PREFACE

As we have traveled in different countries of North and South America, as well as in Europe, we have invariably been asked a number of questions: "How did you brothers in Argentina get into this business of 'discipleship'? When did you begin using the term 'Gospel of the Kingdom', and what do you mean by it? How did it all begin? What was it that brought you together from so many different denominational backgrounds, and what has kept you together for so long?

"How do the many home meetings function throughout the city of Buenos Aires? What is your attitude toward 'church buildings'? What do you mean by the 'unity of the church', and how do you practice it? How do you train your leaders without seminaries or Bible schools? What is your relationship with the other existing Roman Catholic and evangelical groups?"

This book was written as an answer to these and many other questions. Essentially, it is the story of a group of pastors in Buenos Aires: what we discovered together, our joys and victories, our burdens and our trials. It is not a "how-to" book, but rather a simple chronicle of our experiences as the Lord brought us together and taught us something of what the church is all about.

I've made no pretense of making the story more complete or well-rounded than it is in reality. Long ago I tired of exaggerations, distortions, and high pressure salesmanship in the recounting of events. It used to discourage me to read in the Scriptures of the weaknesses and failures of highly esteemed men of God. The word pictures presented in the Bible often leave something to be desired in the lives of such men. But this is reality. Such unbiased reporting now impresses me for its honesty and realism.

I hesitated for a time before accepting the

challenge to write the story. Obviously, it is unfinished. But as I discussed the matter with my colleagues, they all encouraged me to proceed. In reality, it is their story fully as much as it is mine. Friends who have read the developing manuscript have also urged me on and, in fact, have enriched it, sharing anecdotes from their own experiences. Writing it has been a rewarding experience for me personally. It has greatly helped me to develop a keener sense of perspective and evaluation in regards to the framework of our relationships and the nature of our ministry.

One of the most important things I have wanted to communicate to my readers is the need to see all the different aspects and emphases *within the context of the church*. We have consciously sought to avoid becoming top-heavy or overly emphatic about any one issue. We do not see ourselves as a charismatic movement or a discipleship movement or even as an evangelistic or missionary movement. We simply see ourselves as part of the church, the glorious Body of Christ.

My sincere desire is to encourage the reader to open his heart and mind to the Holy Spirit, who is actively renewing the church in our day. We hope that others will be helped by the principles underlined here and encouraged by the narration of our experiences. But we honestly do not expect to see 'carbon-copies' in other cities. We must be flexible, sensitive and obedient to the Holy Spirit. He has an infinite number of ways to work.

Orville Swindoll
Buenos Aires, Argentina

1

WHY CONTAIN IT?

"I will pour out water on the thirsty land and streams on the dry ground."

— Isaiah 44:3

Buenos Aires is a hustling, bustling city of some eleven million people. An ethnic melting pot, for decades it has opened its doors to multitudes of immigrants, mostly from Southern Europe. But not only Italians and Spaniards have settled in the country; thousands of Germans, Russians, Armenians, Jews and others have come seeking refuge from the wars that ravaged Europe. So many have come, in fact, that there have been times during this century when less than half the population of the city were native-born Argentines.

The first impression that the average foreign visitor gets when walking down the streets of this city with its mixture of old and ornate architecture and modern high-rises is that of a typical European metropolis. Some have even been tempted to strike up a conversation with a passerby in German or Italian or English, since the facial features or the dress so clearly indicated such an origin.

But Buenos Aires has not entirely forgotten or forsaken its easy-going, devil-may-care outlook on life. Amid all the fast-moving traffic, people still find time to sit, or walk their dog, or even lie on the grass of the lovely green, tree-shaded parks that turn up every ten or twelve blocks across the entire face of the city.

Beautiful Palermo Park is a dreamer's paradise. Sprawled over scores of acres between the riverside and one of the more sophisticated residential areas, its well-trimmed lawns and attractive lake draw multitudes of city-dwellers from their homes for picnics and outings.

As a matter of fact, this was precisely the scene that appeared to Jorge Himitian in a dream one night in August, 1967. Jorge, young and single, was the pastor of a congregation in one of the less prosperous areas of Buenos Aires. We had met each other only a few months earlier but had already become fast friends. In the dream his family and mine were together for a picnic in the park. While we were chatting together, he heard a voice from heaven commanding him to build dams. Surprised that he should hear such a thing, he looked up to find a giant hand tracing the form of a dam. With that, a huge dam stood erect, right in the middle of the park! Utterly amazed, he asked, "Why should a dam be built here, so far from the river?"

He was startled even more when the voice spoke the second time saying, *"BUILD DAMS!"* Again there was the giant hand shaping a dam. By now he was quite perplexed, inwardly arguing with this disembodied voice, when it spoke the third time in identical fashion. And again the giant hand was at work. Only now he was astounded to find, as he looked toward the river, that the water was rushing into the park in a floodtide that soon had people jumping up into the trees, clambering onto the tops of the cars and crawling up the fences, seeking higher ground. But it was hopeless. The water covered everything, and all were drenched.

When Jorge awoke, he had a deep sense that the dream had come from God, and that through it the Lord was showing him something very important: that a blessing without precedent was to come upon the city of Buenos Aires!

Still, he faced a dilemma. Inwardly, he questioned: "If the floodtide speaks of God's outpoured blessing, then why build a dam to contain it? Wouldn't it be better for it to spill over onto everyone and everything?"

In the afternoon over a cup of tea with a colleague, he shared the dream and his questions. His friend, listening intently, simply smiled and said, "Don't you understand, Jorge? Dams are not just to contain the water, but rather to convert all that pressure into effective energy to get specific tasks done."

Jorge responded immediately. "That's it! That's the message we need to hear!"

As he later shared this insight with several of us who were pastors, we all sensed that the Lord was essentially calling our attention to the intimate relationship between His blessing and His purpose. We needed to understand that His abundant grace upon our lives was for the purpose of getting on toward the goal He had predetermined, and not just to give us a thrill. We saw that too often we and other believers had simply basked in His goodness, not fully appreciating the fact that increased grace means increased responsibility. Later, we would find ourselves with only a memory of "the time when we were all engulfed in the floodtide."

Now God was telling us that His purpose was to bring upon us an unprecedented measure of grace. But more than that, the specific command was that we should begin to take steps — "build dams" — that would assure that this added blessing would serve the Lord's own interests.

Subsequently, we faced another question: What did it mean, in practical terms, to "build dams"? Building obviously meant selecting and putting together materials in an orderly fashion, according to a predetermined plan. We understood that God, in this way, was indicating the specific area of our responsibility in relation to His sovereign purpose.

It was becoming increasingly clear to us that the Lord had determined to pour out His abundant grace upon us. Now we could see that this implied a call to structure our lives and our ministries to fit into His purpose. Then, as His grace flowed, we would be able to channel it in His will.

Step by step, as the months and years passed, we would come to evaluate the tremendous implications in the command to build dams. As yet, we didn't understand much of what was involved. But one thing we did know: something new was happening. God had begun to pour out His Holy Spirit.

2

FIRE ON A DRY PRAIRIE

"He himself will baptize you with the Holy Spirit and fire."

— Matthew 3:11

The house was perhaps 40 or 50 years old, two-story and stately. Since the Darlings had purchased the place several years earlier, they had done a lot of refurbishing and restoring and had it looking quite nice. The large front door opened onto an entrance hall with a small library on the right. Next to that was the staircase leading to the bedrooms upstairs. Then a small utility bathroom and afterwards the kitchen.

On the left side of the hall was a large living room which opened through two glass-paneled doors into the dining room. Beyond that was the gallery, a sort of indoor patio which was really a continuation of the entrance hall, at about the level of the kitchen. This patio had not long since been closed in with glass and aluminum frames, leaving a nice view of the small back yard, dressed in luxuriant shrubs and flowering plants.

Alberto and Alicia Darling were the parents of four growing and active boys. At forty he was an executive in the marketing department of the Coca-Cola Export Corporation, of which he was later to become manager in the Argentine area. Alberto was one of the four sons of an Irishman. Nigel Darling, his father, came to Argentina when the British ran the railroads. As a youth Alberto caught his father's zeal for the Gospel, and had since become one of the more capable and sought-after lay preachers among the Plymouth Brethren.

For years his father had been an elder in a prominent Brethren assembly whose hall was located on Donado Street. Alberto himself was one of four elders who were leading a group in the northern suburban area of Don Torcuato. This had originally begun as an evangelistic outreach from the Donado group, and like many other such groups growing in typical Brethren manner, it had since become a full-fledged assembly, conducting their own baptisms and the regular Sunday celebrations of the Lord's Table.

In spite of his success and prosperity, Alberto was nonetheless dissatisfied with himself and with his church. Too often, it seemed to him, things moved along in a rather hum-drum way without any real evidence of the Lord's hand in it all. Worse still, he knew in his own heart that he was not the man, nor the husband, nor the father, nor the employee, he should be. Still, he held out a hope for release and had recently become more diligent in prayer.

Once, when a friend was visiting him he left with him a copy of Larry Christenson's little pamphlet, *"Speaking in Tongues: A Gift for the Body of Christ"*. This same friend shared with him his own recent experience of the Holy Spirit's fulness. The following day in his downtown office, after reading the booklet, he became so overwhelmed with the sense of God's presence and power that he had to quickly retire to the small bathroom in the hall. There he surrendered completely to God and soon he was praying in a torrent of unknown sounds and rejoicing in the Lord's presence. He knew that release had come and that he had touched something so tremendous, it had the power to transform all things.

Suddenly, it dawned on him that he was still on the earth; and precisely in the office bathroom! As he hurriedly returned to his office, he had the strange sensation that if anyone should speak to him, he would surely answer in some unknown tongue!

In the weeks that followed he became aware

of a growing number of Christians whose hunger for God and for spiritual vitality had led them to the same sort of discovery. And he was avidly devouring everything he could find in print that might throw further light on this new scene. As he learned, he shared with others.

PRAYER MEETINGS OVERFLOW

By March of 1967, a group of 20 or 25 decided to start meeting for prayer on Monday evenings. Alberto immediately offered his home, located in one of the nicer residential areas of Buenos Aires. It was also large enough to accomodate a pretty large crowd. But then, they could hardly have imagined what would happen in the course of the next few months!

Many have said that the fastest means of communication in Latin America is gossip. Anything novel, juicy or scandalous has no need of the press, TV, or radio. The surest way to get a bit of news moving is to get it into the whispering circuit. The thrill of knowing something secret or exclusive is too great to keep it to oneself. So without handbills or bulletins or church announcements, word got around that some Christians, praying in the Darling home for revival, were being filled with the Holy Spirit. It was almost like striking a match to a dry prairie. Every week the number grew.

Things would usually get under way as in a typical church prayer meeting. People would begin arriving between 8 and 8:30 PM, take a seat, lower the head and pray silently. Once a fairly stable nucleus had arrived, someone would spontaneously raise his voice in prayer. This would be followed by another and then another.

But the prayers were different from those heard on Sundays in the church halls. Here the saints were confessing their need, crying out for revival, asking to be filled with the Holy Spirit. They were emboldened to ask, since it was obvious the Lord was meeting others and answering their prayers. The chorus of "Amens" indicated when a common chord or feeling had been touched. There would also be an occasional chorus or well-known hymn that expressed the same sentiment as the prayers. There was a feeling that one could really open up his heart and express his deepest longings, without fearing that he would soon be the subject of a dressing-down by one of the elders.

I think it was this sense of liberty in prayer, coupled with the expectation that God would really hear and do what we asked, that kept folk coming in increasing numbers and from ever greater distances. Many regularly traveled an hour-and-a-half to two hours each way just to be in these prayer meetings where the mercy of God was revealed and His throne could be touched.

Usually the meeting would draw to some kind of finish about 11 PM. Those who had to travel great distances would then slip out, along with others whose curiosity had been satisfied. Invariably, though, a number would stay on chatting, or sharing a problem, or asking counsel of one or more of the pastors and elders that were coming and showing sincere sympathy with what was happening here.

Quite frequently, there were those who specifically asked for prayer and the laying on of hands to be filled with the Holy Spirit. Whenever there was such interest, we usually closed off the living room exclusively for prayer, asking that the others converse in the hall. So it was that week after week, hungry folk were going away after midnight filled and overflowing, drunk on this new and heady wine they had begun to drink.

Naturally, the comments and the exaggerations spread. Word got around that our prayer meetings were conducted with the lights out and that the "laying on of hands" was rather unseemly at times. The rising crescendos of praise and rejoicing made us sound to some like a drunken lot. Others gossipped that the police had closed us down at times, or that there were wild and threatening prophecies. This caused various church leaders to come or send others to spy us out.

Still, the joy and the expectation rose steadily. By the end of the year and on into 1968, every Monday night saw the crowds overflowing the living room into the dining room, with folding chairs filling the entrance hall and the back patio. Young people were seated on the stairway all the way to the top and people were standing in the kitchen, the library, on the front porch and in the back yard.

WHO ARE WE?

By this time, two or three things had made marked changes in the meetings begun earlier in the year. First, the majority had now been filled with the Holy Spirit and thus constituted a stable group of varying denominational backgrounds that was discovering a new and dynamic identity in these Monday gatherings. There were — besides the majority group of Plymouth Brethren — also believers from the Baptists, Mennonites, Christian and Missionary Alliance, Evangelical Union of South America, and a few independents. But something had happened that brought them to share a common, vital, happy experience.

Secondly, the general tone of the meeting had changed. The earlier cries of need and confessions of drouth had given way to shouts of joy, testimonies of victory or answered prayer and exhortations of faith. Worship had become the life-style of the meetings and we were all adoring the Lord. Love was the outstanding hallmark, while the rising tide of faith was causing us all to expect the Lord to do tremendous things.

Finally, some ten or so pastors and elders

that had become regular participants and supporters of the meetings had begun moving more closely together. They seemed to be emerging as the recognized and stable leaders of this new movement for spiritual renewal in the churches and they were frequently sought out for counsel. They shared together in the ministry of the Word which had now become a standard part of the meeting, providing direction and orientation for this growing group of people who were finding a common identity.

Sometimes, when the group of pastors met, they asked themselves such questions as: "Who are we? What are we to become? What is our pastoral responsibility toward these believers?" Until the Lord showed us clearly what we were to do, we were either guessing or surmising on the basis of previous experience or knowledge. Yet, we weren't kept guessing long.

3

BOUND TOGETHER BY THE SPIRIT

"Gather my godly ones to me, those who have made a covenant with me by sacrifice."

— Psalm 50:5

In mid-1967 a visitor from the U.S. told us a story about some well-bred ducks. It seems that the owner of these ducks had them all carefully separated into pens according to their various species. And everything went according to plan until a flood came that caused the water level to rise above the tops of the fences. Once it did, all efforts to keep the species from mixing were vain. What's more, the ducks seemed to thoroughly enjoy the freedom and the new companionships.

We all got the message. The illustration fit our situation perfectly. Most of those attending the meetings in the Darling home had been carefully fenced into ecclesiastical pens. On the whole, relations were friendly between the various evangelical denominations, and even cooperative in certain activities such as a Bible Society program or an evangelistic campaign with well-known figures like Oswald Smith or Billy Graham. However, anything more involved than that tended to be frowned upon.

Probably the legal situation of the churches fomented this sectarian attitude. Since the 1940's a national law had been in effect that required all non-Catholic groups to register with the government, indicating their affiliation, their places of meeting, constituency, doctrinal position and form of government. The law had been rigidly enforced at times and more flexibly at others, depending upon the posture of the changing political authorities. But it did tend to check the growth of spontaneous groups, and to strengthen the position of those having a recognized government permit. Some of the denominational leaders used this permit also as a means to enforce conformity, on the threat of denouncing any who persisted in deviating from tradition.

However, the spiritual vitality of these Monday night gatherings plus the clear indications that there were no intentions of turning the group into another church tended to clear the air of any sectarian struggle. Moreover, those who seemed to be largely responsible for moderating the meetings — always plural, and varied from week to week — were, for the most part, pastors or elders themselves of existing congregations in different parts of metropolitan Buenos Aires.

WELL-KNOWN MINISTER IS FILLED

Some of them had almost impeccable credentials. Augusto Ericsson, for instance, an elder and one of the more effective preachers in a large denomination, had for some twenty years been one of the principal speakers on a daily evangelistic radio program. He was on the staff of editors of a missionary journal and was a much sought-after convention speaker. He was also a member of a widely-traveled evangelistic team that ministered throughout Argentina and had conducted campaigns in other South American and European countries as well. Born in Argentina, of Swedish descent, he turned to Christ in his youth. Before going into the Gospel ministry full-time, he spent several years in business. Augusto is conversant in English as well as Spanish and Swedish and occasionally served as interpreter for visiting preachers from overseas.

He is several years the senior of Alberto Darling and since their wives were sisters, the men were very close to each other, even living just two blocks apart. Thus Augusto learned very soon of Alberto's experience with the Holy Spirit. Having a very warm devotional life and a deep love for the Scriptures, plus a high regard for the integrity of his brother-in-law, he determined to study the matter for himself.

Not long after, alone in his own bedroom, he knelt and asked the Lord to fill him with the Holy Spirit. Soon he was filled to overflowing. Being a cautious man nonetheless, he kept the experience a secret for several weeks while he sounded out his colleagues and sought the Lord for answers to questions he anticipated would be asked. He could hardly have realized that in a few months' time he would be forcibly removed from every denominational responsibility and literally turned out of the church he had effectively served as elder and pastor for so many years.

A REVOLUTIONARY EXPERIENCE

Even earlier than Augusto, another member of the same evangelistic team, Ivan Baker, had felt deep misgivings about the inconsistency between his own biblical fundamentalism and his dearth of spiritual vitality. During the team's tour through Europe he saw tiny congregations more enslaved to tradition than to the Lord, where the names on the church roster had not changed for years. He was told over and over again that the seed of the Gospel had not produced more fruit because the ground was too hard. The really cutting blow, however, was that he had seen other churches, especially Pentecostal groups, in the same towns and cities, that had multiplied in number over recent years. Could the *ground* be the problem then? Or was the problem not rather the *sowers*? He had to find an answer to these questions.

He decided to resign from the team — where he had been both artist and baritone soloist — and give himself to searching the Scriptures for some answers. He also decided to swallow his prejudice and visit some Pentecostal churches near his home. This didn't lead to much at the beginning, especially since the contrasts with his own background were almost too great to handle at the time, but it did begin to open him up to possibilities he had never dreamed of before in his strict fundamentalist upbringing.

Later he led his congregation in Isidro Casanova into a long period of serious study of the book of the Acts of the Apostles. This was followed by some soul-searching prayer meetings that prepared the way for what was to follow. In 1965 Ivan and I met at a spiritual retreat organized by Keith Bentson, then missionary and field director for Overseas Crusades. At that time, Ivan was in the midst of his search which had already made him look unstable and unsettled to many of his friends. They were simply unable to appreciate at the time that it was his deep inner commitment to something permanent and stable, something vital and eternal, which made him appear erratic to them. Inwardly, he knew that he was committed to a search that could not cease until he found the Lord's blessing.

And find it he did! In a life-revolutionizing experience in prayer in 1966 his world was turned upside-down — or rather right-side-up — and he was ready to shout it from the house-tops . . . or at least to all his comrades that would give him a hearing. Soon he was able to lead practically his entire congregation in Casanova into the same spiritual experience. Then nothing could stop them!

Ever since then, Ivan and his followers have seemed to be almost everywhere at once. His tireless energies and his unyielding commitment to make Christ known have made him the beloved leader and pastor of hundreds of men and women, many of whom he has personally led to the Lord and trained in the same heavenly craft.

LARGE FRAME, BIG HEART, BROAD SMILE

Keith Bentson had already served four years as a missionary in Uruguay when he came with his family to Argentina in 1958. From Presbyterian background, he had finished Bible school at BIOLA in Los Angeles. It was there he met Dick Hillis, a former missionary to China and later the founder of a forward-looking mission called Overseas Crusades. After their first term in Uruguay with another mission, Keith and Roberta associated themselves with Hillis' mission and came to Argentina. They first settled in the city of Córdoba, moving to Buenos Aires in 1965.

Keith has always had a gracious manner and winsome way so that he soon won his way into the hearts of many Argentine believers and pastors, especially among the Evangelical Union of South America, the Brethren, the Baptists, and the Christian and Missionary Alliance. He was soon offered the editorship of a little four-page evangelistic monthly — *LA VOZ* — widely distributed by churches throughout the country. At the same time he was busy preaching at special conferences, youth camps, Bible schools, evangelistic crusades and wherever a door was opened. Everywhere his 6-foot-3-inch frame and broad smile made a lasting impression, as his audiences were charmed by his sincerity and his eloquent presentation of the love and truth of the Gospel.

While he was ready to teach others and share anything the Lord had made real to him, he never stopped learning. His heart was always open to the manifold grace and ways of God. Always ready to sit at the feet of a simple farmer or a white-haired theologian, ever seeking to bring out the best and the deepest from a man, never tiring in his open-handed generosity and willingness to share in whatever burden or work was closest to hand, Keith has always been known to the Argentines as a lover of people. His heart and home always seem to be open to seekers after God, or to His wearied servants who need refreshing.

Behind and underneath all these outward expressions is a devoted man of prayer and a lover of the Word of God. Years ago a pastor in the Argentine interior, not particularly fond of Keith, told me, "I really don't go for his ideas or his ways, but you've got to pray with Keith to get to know him." And I shall personally never forget the time I visited in his home to find him devouring large chunks of the Bible daily in order to read the entire Bible through in 30 days.

Keith's ministry often took him far into the interior of the country and almost always in the company of one or two other pastors or promising young men. Together they would preach, teach and pray, ministering to large or small audiences, and always seeking to learn more of what the Lord was doing in different places.

So it was that in 1964 Keith, a Methodist pastor, and a Brethren missionary found themselves in Tucumán province in the far northwest. They had gone to contact local pastors in preparation for some special evangelistic meetings with Argentine evangelist Fernando Vangioni. There they met Jack Schisler, a missionary whose gracious manner and fruitful outreach in the province deeply touched their spirit. Enquiring further, they discovered that Jack credited the success of their witness to an experience of the Holy Spirit's fulness, which not only he but most of the new believers as well had had. His simple and clear testimony moved them all to heart-searching prayer. Upon his return to Córdoba, Keith sought and received the same experience in his own home.

Thereafter he quietly but very effectively shared his new-found joy with intimate friends. Eventually, many other pastors were filled as he prayed for them. It was Keith who later shared Larry Christenson's pamphlet with Alberto Darling.

In the years 1965, 1966 and 1967 Keith organized annual spiritual retreats in the large population centers of Buenos Aires, Mar del Plata, Córdoba and Tucumán. These turned out to have a tremendous impact upon the churches in these areas. Much like John the Baptist's ministry in preparing the hearts of the people for the ministry of Jesus Christ, these retreats were breaking the ground and opening up the way for the spiritual awakening that was to break upon us in force in 1967.

Yet almost as soon as the series of retreats was concluded in 1967, Keith left the country with his family, bound for the U.S.A. and a graduate course at the School of World Mission at Fuller Theological Seminary. Just before their departure in May, he sold or gave away everything since he felt sure his ministry was concluded in Argentina. He even liquidated the mission's assets in the country.

But God had other plans. This beloved man of God, who had through his example and his oral ministry done so much to open up the land to a mighty move of God and to serve as a liaison to bring together key men, could not miss out on all that was to follow. His brothers and sisters in Argentina could never accept his absence as final. But then, we're getting ahead of our story.

A DREAM FULFILLED

Keith and I met in Buenos Aires in 1960 at a literature conference. Though we saw each other again a couple times in the next few years, we really didn't get acquainted until 1965. My wife, Erma Jean, had had a dream some time earlier which seemed to indicate that Keith would at some point have some specific intervention in the direction of our lives. And so it turned out!

In 1965 Keith urged me to attend one of the retreats planned for Córdoba and to bring along some copies of the magazine for believers I had begun publishing the year before. *VISION CELESTIAL* had immediately found acceptance among a broad spectrum of Christians and Keith wanted to give it some promotion. So he asked me to say a few words at the retreat and then copies were given to all those in attendance.

Soon after that he recommended me for some engagements he could not fill himself, which gave me entrance to several of the major denominations. In 1966 and 1967 we worked closely together at the retreats he planned throughout Argentina. Antonio Elias, a Presbyterian pastor from Niteroi, Brazil was the other speaker in 1967. God sovereignly used this man of faith to open the hearts of the Argentine believers to a mighty outpouring of the Holy Spirit. In Buenos Aires, Córdoba and Tucumán, fervent prayer meetings broke out spontaneously following the Saturday evening meetings, and small groups of saints gathered together in their rooms, in the open air, in tents, and under the trees to seek the Lord. Many of these prayer groups continued until the wee hours of the morning and a good number of seekers were filled with the Holy Spirit.

Erma Jean and I had both been raised in Baptist families in Texas and had come to know the Lord at an early age. When we met each other in 1952 we both had a deep hunger for a closer walk with the Lord. Each of us had already been quite concerned about our need for the fulness of the Holy Spirit, but it was not until we were on our honeymoon that we began to seek in earnest. That search was fulfilled in March, 1953, as we overflowed in worship to the Lord.

From that time forward I was converted into an inveterate worshipper.

After a time of pastoring a church in Texas and a brief period with other missionaries in southern Mexico, we moved to Argentina in 1959. I had previously visited the country with another pastor for three months in 1958. For nearly a year and a half we worked in Resistencia, Chaco in the midst of a great spiritual awakening there which had begun under the ministry of missionary Clifford Long. Then in 1961, the Lord clearly led us to the city of Sante Fe, about halfway between Resistencia and Buenos Aires. Most of those years we were involved principally in evangelism and the training of Christian workers until we started publishing the magazine *VISION CELESTIAL* in 1964.

Although filled with the Spirit in a pentecostal church, I never quite fit that mold. Since college days a longing to see and experience the church as the Body of Christ, without sectarian walls, reaching out to all and upward to God, had filled my heart and mind. Somehow I knew that the only way to reach that goal was to learn to follow the leading of the Holy Spirit. So I set myself to learn His ways, to follow His annointing, to hold back when He did not move ahead, to encourage others to press ahead when the Spirit was moving. I knew that obedience to Him was the secret to all spiritual success.

As I became acquainted, one by one, with the men that later were involved in the prayer meetings in the Darling home, I sensed that they, like myself, were God-fearing men who had a sensitive heart and ear to the voice of the Holy Spirit. So convinced were we that the Lord was doing a new and sovereign thing, that my wife and I with our four children moved from Santa Fe to Buenos Aires in 1967. That turned out to be one of the most momentous decisions of our lives.

4

FLOODWATERS

"For all who are being led by the Spirit of God, these are sons of God."

— Romans 8:14

Jorge Himitian, another young pastor active in those meetings in the Darling home from their inception, was destined to have a major part in setting the stage and in sounding out with a clarion voice many of the steps we were to take in the ensuing years. Born in Haifa, Palestine, under British flag and of Armenian stock, his family had to flee when the Israelis invaded the country in 1948. Jorge was just seven and the only son in a family with four daughters. Soon they settled in Argentina where his father and uncle went into business with a relative, wholesaling merchandise to shoe repairmen.

Living in crowded conditions, Jorge spent a good part of every day on the streets learning the ways of the world at an early age. In 1957 Evangelist Vahram Tatikian came to Buenos Aires and had a very successful ministry among the large Armenian community. Jorge came under the conviction of the Holy Spirit and was soundly converted at fifteen. Almost immediately he was out testifying and soon was preaching on the streets and in the plazas which are always full of people. Being quite impressionable and intelligent he soon developed a fiery preaching style and learned to communicate the Gospel effectively and with great conviction.

By the time he finished high school he was already keeping the books in a shoe factory. While studying for the entrance exams into engineering school, the Lord dealt deeply with him about surrendering all his ambitions. Once he had successfully passed the exams he ditched his plans and enrolled instead in the Christian and Missionary Alliance Bible School in the four-year theological course. By the time he began his studies he already had several years of experience preaching and had developed a close walk with the Lord. The school rector, Myron Voth, told some of us later that Jorge had the highest IQ of anyone who had gone through the school and that his devotional life was always an example to the rest of the students.

Jorge and I first met on Jan. 1, 1967 at a Youth for Christ camp where we had been invited to speak. We hit it off well right away, each having heard of the other and anxious to get acquainted personally. We discovered we were on the same wavelength, both being deeply concerned to see a spiritual awakening in the churches. He was pastoring a congregation in Villa Soldati (within the capital city of Buenos Aires), and I was still living in Santa Fe.

I invited him to Santa Fe for meetings in March and then he arranged for me to be with his group in Buenos Aires in August after we got settled in the area. That was a clear turning point, both for him and for myself, as well as for the believers in Soldati. The one week of meetings stretched into five, and we had visitors from all over Buenos Aires. No meeting began later than 8 PM and none was over before midnight.

There were no special efforts to string out the meetings, for we tried over and again to conclude around 10:30. But as soon as the closing prayer was finished, someone would break out praying spontaneously, then another would strike up a chorus, then a testimony or a request for prayer. And so it went on until midnight. People of the church that had before been nervous when a meeting lasted more than an hour and a half, were now in every single meeting. What's more, they were distressed to find that after four hours we had to conclude!

TOO MUCH WATER

Among those who attended night after night were students from the Baptist Seminary in Buenos Aires. One of them had an unforgettable experience. After one of the meetings we were praying for those who wanted to be filled with the Holy Spirit. He was crying out, almost in agony of soul, "Oh God, I'm so thirsty! Oh God, I want to drink from Your river . . . Fill me tonight!" As we laid hands on him in prayer, the Lord so filled him that he didn't know what to do with himself! He gushed, he shouted, he praised God in other tongues, he jumped up and down for sheer joy.

The next night he was in the meeting again, and it was impossible to contain him. As we worshipped the Lord, this mighty heavenly river burst from his innermost being, and he shouted out, "Oh God, what do I do with all this water?"!

During those weeks the Lord was transforming the whole congregation. Many were filled with the Holy Spirit, most were opening up to worship and we were all learning new choruses which seemed to lift us to the portals of glory. One night I taught them a chorus which was slow and worshipful, and which seemed to express exactly what everyone was sensing:

We worship and adore thee,
Bowing down before thee,
Songs of praises singing,
Hallelujahs ringing:
Hallelujah, Hallelujah, Hallelujah, Amen.

We sang it again and again, perhaps fifteen or twenty times, as hearts were melted in the presence of divine glory, holiness and love.

After the meeting, Jorge's father was visibly upset. When Jorge enquired as to the reason, he said that we had ruined a beautiful chorus by singing it so many times. Jorge tried to soothe the troubled waters by saying something about the fact that since all were learning together the meaning of true worship, it would not do to be too critical at this point. That seemed to take care of the problem for the moment.

The following week, his father was filled with the Holy Spirit during the time of worship one evening. He sank to his knees while the rest remained standing, and he started singing a song all his own. When everyone else stopped, he continued, absolutely lost in worship and adoration. For the longest time he sang and praised the Lord in tongues and in spontaneous words of love that sprang from his grateful heart. Never again did he complain about a chorus that we sang over and over!

He was fluent in six languages and had remarked at one time that he saw no need for tongues in his case, since he could already praise the Lord in any one of several languages. That theory too went out the window after that night in Soldati!

CULTIVATING A HEARING HEART

It was during those days that Jorge had the dream about building dams, which was related in the opening chapter. That revelation was to have a formative effect on the course of events in most of our lives for years to come. Among the pastors meeting together on Saturday mornings we talked over its implications in the light of what was happening in the Monday night meetings. We all agreed that there was certainly a sense of God's presence with us, but there was not a very clear sense of direction as to where we were going. We felt that one of the things most needed was a nucleus of men "tuned in" to the moving of the Holy Spirit, men who could cooperate intelligently and in faith as He worked among us, men that were preeminently "men of the Spirit".

He concluded that our first significant step would be to organize a retreat to which would be invited only men who were attending the Monday gatherings and who were responsible for some area of leadership in their own church groups. The purpose would be to expose these men to an intense course of "walking in the Spirit" which would last about a week. The date was set for early October (1967). The first three meetings were held on Tuesday, Wednesday and Thursday evenings in the Darling home. Then on Friday evening we all went out to a Salvation Army campground in Benavidez, just north of Buenos Aires, where we stayed until Sunday night.

The next detail to be settled had to do with the ministry for the retreat. After some discussion, it was agreed that two brothers would be invited to speak, and each would have six sessions to develop his subject. I was urged to speak on the anointing of the Holy Spirit, and in the first few sessions we traced that anointing in the Old and New Testaments. Out of that I drew several lessons and then suggested some conclusions applicable to our time and situation. In the final sessions we put these lessons into practice as we worshipped and prayed together, seeking to cultivate a "hearing heart".

For the remainder of the ministry we decided to invite a man known only to a few of the group, but who seemed to be a very sensitive person, with considerable experience in the workings of the Holy Spirit in spite of his relative youth. Juan Carlos Ortiz was already developing a reputation for diligence and enterprise in his growing Assembly of God congregation in the heart of Buenos Aires. Jorge spoke highly of him, mentioning that Juan Carlos was also watching us closely to see what the Lord was doing among us.

We asked Juan Carlos to teach on the gifts of the Holy Spirit. He was a master as he unfolded his subject with apt illustrations and amazing ability to clarify issues that had formerly seemed obscure. In a word, he won our hearts. We did not realize then that a similar thing was happening to him. His own roots were pentecostal, and now he was sensing a deep work of the Holy Spirit in this group of men, not a single one of which came from that background. He was later to testify openly that this series of events and contacts brought about a real revival in his own life. One thing is clear above all else: from that time forward our hearts were knit together as one.

OTHER PASTORS INVOLVED

There were other pastors in that group that began to meet and share together on Saturday mornings from August, 1967 forward. There was Angel Negro, a promising young minister among the Plymouth Brethren, who was developing a warmly appreciated preaching and teaching gift, especially in youth conferences, as well as in his own congregation in a suburban area. Angel had been deeply touched in the retreat where Antonio Elias had spoken and was subsequently filled with the Holy Spirit.

Jorge Pradas had migrated to Argentina from near Barcelona, Spain twelve years earlier. Being gifted in the scenic arts, he had helped in the production of several films. Also a poet, he had seen much of his poetry published, both in books and in Christian periodicals. An eloquent speaker, he was in growing demand for Christian conferences around the country, and in Quilmes he was active in a local assembly. Pradas had been filled with the Holy Spirit earlier in the year while visiting in our home in Santa Fe.

And there were others. Pastors, seminary students, elders, Sunday School teachers, and simple hungry children of God. We have always felt that one of the reasons the foundation was so well laid in those early meetings in the Darling home, was because of the spiritual preparation of these folk God was getting together each week. They were doing serious business with God, for they knew that their decisions would affect many others.

Certainly it was evident the Lord was getting us together. There were too many clear indications of that for us to doubt. Obviously, many things were yet to be ironed out. All of us held out high hopes that our congregations and wider circle of church relationships would open up to this dynamic move of the Holy Spirit. We wanted to see the church at large experience a spiritual awakening and renewal. We hoped things would spread out rapidly. Yet soon it became clear that first some simple and basic things had to be settled. Our commitment to the Lord must be absolute; it must be clear to us that He was in charge.

Very soon the Lord was to deal further with Jorge Himitian and use him to shake a broad cross-section of the church in Argentina. Spiritual revelation would be followed by spiritual revolution.

5

TRUMPET SOUND

"For if the bugle produces an indistinct sound, who will prepare himself for battle?"

— I Corinthians 14:8

As a young lad Jorge Himitian frequented the Salvation Army meetings near his home, and was there enchanted by the band. Something about a band stirred his vivacious personality. From the time he was nine until the age of fourteen he studied violin, at the insistence of his parents. But though it gave him a basic understanding of music, he never did really take to the instrument.

By the time he was sixteen he began playing the trumpet, and soon thereafter was using his horn to draw a crowd in the open air meetings on the street corners and in the plazas of downtown Buenos Aires. And when the young band of evangelists later traveled around the country and into Uruguay, Jorge was always there with his trumpet.

Although he has never considered himself an accomplished musician, he certainly is a lover of good music. And creative too: several of the choruses and hymns we sing were composed by him. Jorge seems to be equally comfortable with a guitar, on the keyboard of a piano or accordion, or with a trumpet. Yet in the minds of most of us that know him well, the trumpet is the instrument we associate with him, since it seems to exactly match his style and temperament.

The trumpet, unlike a string or keyboard instrument, sounds only one note at a time. If that note is sounded with precision and with strength, it usually stands out above all other instruments in an orchestra. In spiritual matters Jorge has always been concerned that whatever note is communicated should be sounded with clarity and with conviction.

JESUS IS LORD!

One Monday morning in January, 1968, Jorge and I were in the office of the publishing firm we had recently begun. We were chatting together over his sermon the day before in his own congregation. It was a message on the lordship of Christ which had stirred him deeply as he was preparing it. Being quite sound in evangelical theology, he had for years believed in the truth of Christ as Lord. But like so many others, he had more or less adopted the position that to be saved one has to simply confess Jesus Christ as his Savior; whereupon his sins are forgiven. Subsequently, often at some crisis point, there would come a recognition that He is Lord. That is to say, in the minds of many, there is no direct relationship between the lordship of Christ and their experience of salvation.

This is precisely the premise that Jorge was now questioning. As he focused on Romans 10:9, 10, it seemed as clear as a bell that salvation is the direct result of acknowledging Jesus Christ as Lord. So he asked himself, "Then where did we get the idea that one needs only to confess Christ as Savior? Why is the confession of His lordship postponed to a later experience?" At this point, all kinds of bells and buzzers began to go off inside him.

He decided that before allowing his imagination to run away with him, he should first investigate the way that Jesus evangelized. What did he preach? How did he win souls? As he researched the Gospels he was literally amazed at what he found. Jesus began his public ministry with a proclamation and a command: "The time is fulfilled, and the kingdom of God is at hand; repent and believe in the gospel" (Mark 1:15).

When he came upon Simon Peter and his brother Andrew by the seaside, he issued a command: "Follow me, and I will make you fishers of men" (Matt. 1:19). To Levi the publican, his word was brief and imperative: "Follow me" (Luke 5:27). When he saw Zaccheus in the sycamore tree in Jericho, it was much the same: "Hurry and come down, for today I must stay at your house" (Luke 19:5). With the rich young ruler, it was more than he could take; yet Jesus made not a single concession: "Sell all that you possess, and distribute it to the poor, and you shall have treasure in heaven; and come, follow me" (Luke 18:22).

The authoritative nature of Jesus' preaching seemed foreign to the watered-down language to which most evangelicals are accustomed. Almost fearful of too radical a departure from tradition, Jorge knew he had to have a solid scriptural basis for what he sensed was coming. Feeling innately that the crux of the question revolved around the *Lordship* of Christ, while the bulk of the Gospel sermons he had heard and preached himself centered upon the *Saviorhood* of Christ, he set out to check the epistles to see how the early Christians understood the relationship between those two terms. To his amazement, he found the word *Savior*, with reference to Christ, appeared only a handful of times; whereas *Lord* appeared more than 300 times!

When he delved further into the meaning of the word *Lord*, especially in the light of Paul's teaching in Philippians 2:5-11, the truth began to loom very large in his thinking. In the understanding of the early Christians, the term *Lord* (*kyrios* in Greek) was something like the sum of Chief, Owner, Boss, Sovereign, Maximum Authority, all rolled into one. It was used exclusively to refer to a person with vast authority and property and — especially — owner of many slaves. Most importantly, it referred to the Roman Emperor, considered divine and the owner of all under his rule. To address a person with the term *kyrios* implied allegiance, subjection, the position of a bondslave.

UNCOMFORTABLE TERMINOLOGY

One point came across with special clarity in his research: in the same way that there can be no husband without a wife, no parents without a child, there can be no lord without a slave. Therefore, it followed that once the Lordship of Christ was established, the role of the bondslave had to be clarified. This term also occurs frequently in the New Testament, but because it is commonly translated *servant,* its significance is obscured, especially to our 20th century mentality.

Every bondslave in the first century — and there were many — knew well that his master's desire was his command. A proper attitude on his part was frequently expressed as: "What does my lord desire of his servant?" And it was this attitude that Jorge saw was largely lacking in 20th century Christianity. We rather tend to barter and reason and argue with the Lord, instead of obeying him implicitly. With such an attitude, we can hardly refer to him properly as Lord. So the term makes us uncomfortable.

The results of this lack of submission are self-evident. The word of God is not taken seriously; his commands go unheeded; his right to govern our lives is questioned. Instead, we find humanistic philosophies abounding in the churches; ambitious programs that are the invention of men; lack of concern for prayer which in any case has lost its effectiveness; and a general loss of spiritual vitality.

What a contrast with the early Christians! Many literally left all to follow Jesus. Some paid with their lives for their loyalty to Christ. The consciousness of their spiritual need and their total surrender to the Lord Jesus bound them together in tightly-knit fellowships that shone as bright lights in a dark, pagan world motivated by self-seeking, insecurity or fears.

The simple Gospel message began to come across in bold relief: All of us have sinned and turned our backs on God, preferring to manage our lives as we please. Jesus came to live as a man under God's authority on this earth, to restore God's original plan for men; to show us that peace and joy are the products of obeying God and living in right relationship with Him. Because of His total submission to his Father's will, He was victorious over temptation, over demons, over deception. Then He willingly gave up that perfect life for us to free us from our bondage to sin, ignorance and egotism. He shed His blood for us in order to reconcile us to God.

Therefore, we must repent of our sin, rebellion and independence, and acknowledge Jesus Christ as our Lord and come under his rule, submitting our lives totally and unreservedly to Him in obedient service. In doing so, we become His property, His people, His possession, and He molds us together in His own image and as effective instruments for carrying forward His eternal purpose, through His Holy Spirit who lives in us.

THE GOVERNMENT OF GOD
HERE AND NOW

As these truths began to fit into place, the fuller picture started coming into focus. Jesus preached about a kingdom, a government. He called His message "the Gospel of the kingdom of God". Now, in the context that was taking shape in Jorge's mind, God's government began to make sense; not as something merely relegated to the future or the eternal state, but rather something of extremely important relevance for "here and now".

He knew within himself that he had never

preached this Gospel of the kingdom. But he could begin to see what a powerful instrument it could be in the Lord's hand; what a challenge it could issue to careless, indifferent sinners; and what hope it could engender in the hearts of the sin-sick and helpless.

So it was that he began his exposition of this Gospel of the kingdom of God on that memorable Sunday in January, 1968. He continued over the next two Sundays as well. Then Ortiz asked him to give the same series at his own congregation on Hidalgo Street. Soon word spread to the interior of the country and Jorge found himself preaching the Gospel of God's government in the city of Santa Fe, then in the provinces of Tucuman, Salta, and Chaco.

As he preached, the conviction grew that this uncluttered, unhindered Gospel was in truth the "power of God unto salvation to everyone who believes." The number of messages grew as well. The original three had now been enlarged into a series of six. Early the following year, having polished and refined his presentation, he went through the entire series on successive Monday nights. This time they were recorded, and taped copies began to circulate. Finally, in 1974 we got the entire series into print as a book.

Although Jorge would introduce minor variations from time to time, according to what he sensed as areas of special need in his audiences, normally he would develop his subject under three main topics. First, he would show that Jesus Christ is the Lord of our personal lives; second, that He is Lord of the church; and finally, that He is Lord over all the universe.

Under the topic of Christ's lordship in the church he unfolded the bulk of his teaching. He began by giving a panoramic overview of the development of the idea of the kingdom in the Old Testament, continuing with the thought in the Jewish mind in the period of the Gospels. He showed how this thought was central in Jesus' message as well as in that of His apostles. He then pointed up the two governments that are diametrically opposed to each other: the kingdom of self where all live in darkness and the kingdom of Christ where all is light and all delight to do His will. He spoke of the kingdom community as seen in the early church, and concluded with a careful and extensive definition of the Gospel of the kingdom.

Jorge's style has always been clear and practical, expressing involved concepts in easy-to-understand language with forcefulness. He put a lot of study into the preparation and development of these messages. Yet he has always contended that the core of the truth came to him by "revelation"; that is to say, a definite work of the Spirit of God, illuminating and clarifying scriptural truth to his mind and heart This impressive combination of spiritual enlightenment, solid biblical exegesis and eloquent delivery laid the foundation for the next important step in our journey toward renewal and restoration.

6

READY TO OBEY

"All authority has been given to me in heaven and on earth. Go therefore and make disciples of all the nations."

— Matthew 28:18, 19

The pastors meeting together on Saturday mornings and leading the larger Monday night meetings had among them considerable aggregate experience in evangelism. Already mentioned were Jorge Himitian's years of street preaching and Augusto Ericsson's work on the radio and with the evangelistic team. Ivan Baker had a major part in the beginning of several congregations and was a constant personal worker and soul-winner. Alberto Darling had won a number to the Lord in the area where he was ministering.

Ortiz had conducted large evangelistic campaigns in many parts of Argentina with outstanding results. And in Santa Fe and Chaco provinces I had personally trained scores of believers in evangelistic work, leading them into one village after another where we gave a Gospel witness in every home.

Yet all of us were concerned over the lack of effectively building the church. Even with intense activity in evangelism, too little of the raw material gathered together actually went into God's building. We could see from our own experience that the answer was not simply to increase the follow-up. Ortiz had a sophisticated program in high gear in his assembly, largely learned from personal contacts in the United States. But it required an office staff, considerable expenditure on printed materials and large and frequent mailings. The whole thing seemed unnatural and foreign to the New Testament setting we read about in the book of Acts.

We knew in our hearts that any program that depended on experts, office staff or expensive equipment would only bog down the real work of the church in the long run. What's more, it put such a program beyond the reach of simple believers or poor congregations. No; the answer had to be simple and practical. It had to be applicable in every situation; among the poor as well as the rich; under persecution as well as in times of liberty and prosperity; in the midst of spiritual revival and in struggling new outreaches; among professionals and with blue-collar workers.

SIMPLE AND UNSOPHISTICATED

Our initial steps in a new direction were not especially noteworthy, but as we moved ahead the way became clearer. Our own experiences, our mutual sharing, our study and a deep concern to be more fruitful all combined to move us forward. Ivan and I had both garnered some valuable lessons from contact with the "Navigators". We had gone through their Scripture memory course and were persuaded of the validity of their strong emphasis on man-to-man personal relationships for spiritual nourishment.

Especially Ivan could see tremendous possibilities in the Navigator plan of one Christian winning and training one other person in the course of a year and then the two repeating the process in successive years. At the end of two years there would be four, in three years eight, in four years sixteen, and so on. He pointed out that numerical growth would be slow at first, but after ten years there would be over 1000. In 20 years there would be one million and in 30 years a billion.

Even if the plan be defaulted for over-simplicity or mechanical rigidity, the principle was clear. And to Ivan's pragmatic mind, it offered noteworthy advantages. It could be easily taught and simply illustrated. It required no special equipment or funds, nor even a lot of free time. No experts were necessary and no high pressure tactics. On the contrary, such elements could prove to be counterproductive.

As Ivan studied and prayed, interceding for his flock in Casanova, more light was shed on his pathway. Gradually, he came to realize that, until now, he had always taken his evangelistic methods from the book of Acts onward. Suddenly, the words of Jesus to his disciples in John 20:21 acquired new meaning: "As the Father has sent me, I also send you." Now it dawned on him: go back to the four Gospel accounts. See how the Father sent Jesus, and how Jesus sent His disciples.

As he went through the Gospels, he was struck by the extremely simple, unsophisticated methods he found. He realized that anyone could learn these things and apply them easily. In his own words, here are the essential lessons he discovered in the four Gospels:

1) Jesus did not give sermons so much as He gave Himself.

2) Jesus went to the people; He did not ask them to come and hear him.

3) He accepted the circumstances as He found them: seaside, mountain, well, home, etc. His major pronouncements were made in the simplest circumstances.

4) He only sought those that were hungry and thirsty after righteousness.

5) He made a selection of disciples. He never tried to keep those who wanted to leave. Then he sent out those selected on specific missions.

6) He required only three years to form twelve apostles.

7) They were apparently quite unprepared when He sent them. His dependence was

obviously on the Holy Spirit to complete the work necessary in them.

Someone, then, had to apply these principles and provide a kind of model that would encourage others. Ivan decided to get the believers in Casanova involved. First, He called them to prayer and encouraged them to seek the Lord for greater fruitfulness and effectiveness in their witness to the lost. At a particular Saturday night prayer meeting several Scripture texts were brought before the group for consideration:

— the words of Jesus in Matthew 4:19, "Follow me, and I will make you fishers of men."

— His statement in John 10:27, "My sheep hear my voice, and I know them, and they follow Me."

— the passages in Mark 8:34, 35 and Luke 14:25-33, which illustrate the strict requirements which Jesus laid down for all who would follow Him.

"TELL US HOW IT'S DONE"

Then on Thursday evening he preached the Gospel to the congregation in these terms. But they balked. Try as he might, even after months he could not get them to accept either the basic conditions Jesus laid down for discipleship, nor the personal responsibility for others that was essential for effective evangelism. They had become too comfortable, too accustomed to church leaders whose special call, special training or special grace equipped them to bear most of the burden of evangelistic outreach as well as subsequent spiritual nurture and edification. Ivan was frustrated and grieved.

By early 1968 he and his wife Gloria decided upon a rather radical departure. The two of them would begin sharing the Gospel intensively with their immediate neighbors, win some to the Lord, gather them together, baptize them in water and teach them the Word; all this without so much as informing the believers in Casanova. In the meantime, things would continue in Casanova as before.

The Lord blessed the new effort from the beginning. Starting with the family next door, they won the elder son and his fiancée, followed by his brother and then the mother. All were baptized between May and November that year. Around the corner they found another interested young couple and then another and another. Soon there was a nice little group dropping in for tea, for early morning times of prayer, for Bible study and for occasional counseling. Often on Sunday mornings they would meet together briefly and then spread out for witnessing.

After six or eight months they had a fairly stable group of about a dozen. Then Ivan suggested to them the next step in his revolutionary plan. During all this time he had continued to pastor the group in Casanova and to seek in vain the reorientation of the saints according to the aforementioned plan. He and Gloria had quietly gone about their work in their own neighborhood, with results that totally convinced them of the feasibility of such a program. Now it was time to introduce the group from their home to the congregation in Casanova.

The major meeting in Casanova was held on Sunday evenings. So Ivan and Gloria arranged for all the new believers from their home group to attend the meeting in Casanova on a Sunday evening. At the appointed hour, along with those who regularly attended, the new people started arriving. The older ones were naturally elated, thinking that this was evidence that some folk in the neighborhood of the church hall were at last showing an interest in the Gospel.

When Ivan introduced them all as new converts that he and Gloria had been winning in their own neighborhood, and the older believers discovered that these "babes" in Christ were well oriented and spiritually healthy, some of them already having won relatives and friends to Christ, the Casanova Christians were both amazed and ashamed. At the close of the meeting, one of the elders came up to Ivan, confessed his hardness of heart and his shame, then crossed his hands in front of him as if to be bound, and said simply, "Tell us how it's done, Ivan. We are ready to obey." It was the dawning of a new day in Casanova!

IT TAKES TIME

About this time Ortiz called Ivan at his home one day and queried: "How should we preach the Gospel?" The answer came to Ivan after hanging up: "Go and make disciples." He sat down at his desk and began to develop on paper the steps that were gradually becoming clear in the light of his own experience. He was beginning to understand that this plan introduced a complete change in his pastoral methods. It wasn't enough to *win* people. They then had to be *formed*. He discovered it was necessary to communicate, not just precepts, but also living examples.

In order to learn to do something, more than instruction is necessary. We must also practice. So Ivan realized that his error in Casanova had been that he was simply teaching theory. Now it was necessary to provide also the context for working it out in practice. And this would require a greater investment of time.

He asked himself how much time he would have to invest in a person in order to form him as a disciple. After weighing different factors he came up with a tentative answer of about five hours weekly over a period of three months. At that point he realized he could never do it alone. Some major changes would have to come in the ministry of the church. He knew then that he would have to train men to train men to train men.

After the elders in Casanova told Ivan they were ready to get in the harness and learn, Ivan determined to spend three months with them intensively. He then divided all the willing workers in the congregation under the three elders.

The next problem discovered in Casanova was the lack of time available to concentrate on making disciples. There were too many meetings! This, of course, was not a problem with the group of neighbors that Ivan and Gloria had won to the Lord, for their growth from the beginning had been based upon relationships rather than on a schedule of meetings. Time and again they were finding that the traditional church structure posed one of the biggest problems to progress in discipleship.

Throughout 1968 Ivan and Jorge had been sharing these concerns and discoveries with the group of pastors. We were all talking about the Lordship of Christ, the Gospel of the kingdom and about making disciples. But we really had not yet synchronized or coordinated these things precisely in our minds. So many things were happening at once!

7

CROWDED HALLS AND ANOINTED MESSENGERS

"Many were gathered together, so that there was no longer room, even near the door; and He was speaking the word to them."

— Mark 2:2

Interest in the Monday night meetings was growing rapidly. Early in the year 1968 we had rented a nice hall in the commercial center of Buenos Aires for these gatherings, since it was obvious the crowds were too large to continue in the Darling home. The Jewish owner of the hall was happy to have us since hardly anyone ever rented a hall on Mondays. He had three hundred chairs which seemed sufficient to begin with, but it wasn't long before we had them all filled. Then he purchased two hundred more. By mid-1969 six hundred or more were jamming into the place every Monday night. It was literally wall-to-wall people! One person made the comment that it was so crowded that when you raised your hands in praise, you couldn't get them down again!

It seemed that people were coming from everywhere. Included were many well-known church leaders and pastors who would slip in late and stand around the back wall.

By this time there was a more or less standard format. Different pastors would alternate in leading the meetings, and for the first hour or so there would be victorious praise and loving worship to the Lord. A new chorus or Scripture verse set to music was taught at the rate of one or two every week. Occasionally, during this time of worship newcomers would be filled with the Spirit, although more frequently this would happen at the close of the meeting.

An offering would be received without any pressure whatever, and was always more than the immediate need. From this excess fund we often helped pastors who were going through a rough place, or helped to underwrite the expenses of a spiritual retreat, or paid the fare of a brother traveling in ministry. Ortiz had given a series of messages on Christian stewardship while we were still in Darling's home, which had so moved the people to tithe and give beyond the tithe, that there was never a financial problem.

There was always a time of ministry from the Word of God. Hardly ever did anyone preach less than an hour. It was far more common for the ministry to continue for ninety minutes or so. Interest was intense throughout. There seemed to be a prophetic anointing upon those who taught or preached. We all had the sense that God was pulling back the veil and giving us a glimpse of heavenly things.

Of course, there was an occasional "dry run", but these were indeed rare. The tides of faith were high. Hearts were hungry and grace was abundant. There was unity among the pastors, even though some were being sorely tried through tensions in the creaking wineskins of their traditional ecclesiastical structures. It was clearly a "day of God's power". The Lord was renewing his church.

A THREAT OR A HOPE?

Somehow we knew that God was interested in more than church renewal, more than a charismatic awakening. Already we were being seen by many as a threat to some of the existing churches, rather than as a hope for revival, as we tended to view ourselves, obviously with some naiveté. Many of the Christians involved with us were being accused of turning pentecostal; whereas Ortiz was being accused by his

Assembly of God colleagues of joining the Plymouth Brethren!

Everyone wanted to tag us with some convenient label. Since we frequently referred to a present-day move of the Holy Spirit in Argentina to bring renewal to the church, we soon got tagged with that name: the "spiritual renewal movement", or more simply, "the movement". That was as good as any, we supposed; in any case, we never adopted any official label.

The sum of our organization was limited to whatever was necessary to function with decency and order. A treasurer for the Monday gatherings was appointed and the funds were managed jointly by the group of pastors. Whenever special conferences or a retreat was planned, a functional committee was established for the duration of the event, ceasing thereafter. The various congregations continued to be autonomous or denominationally organized, according to the preference of each group. There was no effort to bring them together under any kind of umbrella organization.

As the pastors met together on Saturday mornings for prayer and comparing of notes, many of us sensed the need for clearer direction as to the shape of our growing responsibilities toward this dynamic group of people so willing to follow. Moreover, we strongly felt that the direction had to be toward greater and more effective evangelism. We began concentrating our prayers in that area, asking the Lord for wisdom and enlightenment of the Holy Spirit.

ANOTHER RETREAT PLANNED

Since 1965 many of the major steps forward were taken or clearly indicated to us as a group through the spiritual retreats held at various times. These were to continue to serve a vital function for years to come. So at this point it seemed logical for us to think in terms of planning another retreat and asking the Lord to give clear direction to his people through that means. We had just learned that Keith Bentson, after seventeen months in the U.S., would be visiting Argentina in October, so we set the date for the retreat to coincide, and made plans for Keith to be one of the speakers.

The choice for the other speaker fell unanimously upon Juan Carlos Ortiz, one of our own number who had been deeply moved like the rest of us to seek the Lord for orientation. As the date drew nearer our expectancy mounted. We were sure God would give us just what we needed.

Ortiz had been one of the first to invite Jorge to give the series on the Kingdom of God to his own congregation, and had become fully persuaded of the validity and timeliness of this truth. He had also spent considerable time with Ivan and was moving in much the same direction as he, seeking to reorient his people, and was already seeing rather rapid numerical growth. Ortiz has an exceptionally agile mind and a remarkable ability to communicate with eloquence whatever facet of truth is upon his heart. Therefore it seemed most fitting that he should expound to us the Word of the Lord at this time.

In his first message — on the general subject of evangelism — he talked about the necessary basis for effective outreach: the spiritual climate of the church. He compared the church to a married couple; where there is harmony and love, there will surely be offspring. He pointed out that winning others to Christ ought not be some special effort of the believers, but the normal everyday way of life.

His second message was an unfolding of the Gospel of the kingdom, with emphasis on Jesus Christ as King and Lord. He pointed up the need for an unconditional surrender to Christ from the very first day of conversion, and the need for a clear and authoritative presentation of the Gospel by the church.

Next he spoke on the scriptural method of evangelism: making disciples. Beginning with an exposition of Matthew 28:18-20, he emphasized the three words, GO... MAKE... DISCIPLES. The broad outline had come from Ivan but the style and illustrations were unmistakably his own! As he preached, we laughed, we cried, we came under conviction and we surrendered to the Lord. We knew we would never be the same again. I think that the most significant thing that was indelibly impressed upon our hearts and minds was the need for each of us to assume personal responsibility to make disciples, not just to win souls.

In his final discourse, Ortiz shared the testimony of his Hidalgo congregation over the past several months, the changes and adjustments that were taking place and the new materials and methods they were developing in their initial efforts to make practical application of the truths he had been expounding.

Keith Bentson's ministry filled out the program with apt illustrations of varied experiences in evangelism from Argentina, Mexico, the United States and elsewhere. His words were encouraging and faith-building, amply supporting the basic thesis that Ortiz was developing in alternating sessions. All eight messages of these two men of God were published the following year in a book in Spanish entitled: *"AND THIS GOSPEL SHALL BE PREACHED"*.

A few years ago I heard Dr. Donald Hoke in Lausanne, Switzerland, during a conference at the Youth With a Mission headquarters, just a few weeks prior to the great conference on evangelism sponsored there by the Billy Graham Association in 1974. Referring to the vitality of spiritual movements throughout the course of church history, he said that we usually find three outstanding types of men who come to the fore as mutually complementary elements: the theoretician or theologian, the pragmatist, and the articulator. While such positions are never exclusive — there is always some overlapping — these three kinds of ministry were becoming more evident among us.

Jorge Himitian was developing a solid stance as our outstanding thinker, our theologian. Ivan Baker's insistence upon working everything out in practice brought him to the front as the activist, the pragmatist. And hardly anyone would question that, even when we have never lacked capable preachers and teachers, Juan Carlos Ortiz was evidently the outstanding speaker, the articulator. So by late 1968 the complementary relationships between the pastors was beginning to take clearer shape. Yet the Lord purposed to unite us even more profoundly.

8

TORTUGUITAS AND NEHEMIAH

"Then they said, "Let us arise and build." So they put their hands to the good work."

— Nehemiah 2:18

Early in 1969, Pablo Pachalian, a young Baptist pastor in the city of Pergamino, invited Jorge and me for a series of meetings. He had been filled with the Holy Spirit a couple years earlier and his warm heart and joyful ministry were bringing spiritual renewal to his congregation.

There was a delightful flow in the meetings and we enjoyed the fellowship with the Christians there, but Jorge and I were especially grateful for the opportunity afforded to have some time together for intensive conversation and prayer. Things were brewing inside us that we needed to talk over.

By this time both of us had had quite a bit of itinerant ministry in churches, youth camps, spiritual retreats, Bible school conferences, denominational conventions and leaders' seminars. It was clear to us that the Lord was moving across all kinds of ecclesiastical boundaries. There was hardly an evangelical group in the country that was not experiencing in some measure a fresh breeze from heaven. Some were firmly resisting, but many were welcoming it and finding a new joy in their walk, a new hunger for the Scriptures and a new victory in their prayers.

One thing was abundantly clear to us both as we pondered the significant period of time we were living in: God was doing something above and beyond all our traditions, our expectations and our organizations. We could see that this out-

1968 — Author in the middle, Himitian and Ortiz to the right, Schisler is to the far left.

1971 — Ivan Baker is to the left, Keith Bentson on the right.

1969 — Pastors' Retreat at Soldini.

In 1971, Orville visited the Trappist Monastery in Azul.

This is a 1972 photo of Alberto Darling and his wife Alicia, with his mother and three of four sons.

pouring of the Holy Spirit was not for the purpose of making us better Baptists, Methodists, Anglicans or Plymouth Brethren. This might be one of the initial effects, but it could hardly be the goal. We could see that the Holy Spirit simply was not interested in building denominational structures. He is building the Church, the Body of Christ, a people bound together in a spiritual union that transcends all sectarian differences.

ECCLESIASTICAL STRESS

Yet we felt no hostility toward the different ecclesiastical structures where we found ourselves ministering from time to time. We rejoiced to see the Lord gloriously at work among them, bringing people to Himself, building up the saints, encouraging pastors and church leaders, and filling Christians with the Holy Spirit. And we were happy for whatever part we could play in the process.

We urged the believers to remain in their own congregations rather than to begin an exodus in search of 'greener pastures'. We knew how illusory the search often turns out to be.

In all honesty, however, it is necessary to say that many did leave their traditional structures. Some found themselves under intense pressure to be quiet and conform. Others were plainly told to leave. And some simply refused to stay in a situation where they felt they were starving spiritually.

Experience has taught us that it is most difficult, if not impossible, to judge who is right in such cases. Often there are unbecoming attitudes on both sides, or tactical errors, or bad judgment at a crucial point.

On the negative side, unethical conduct should never be commended. On the positive side, the Holy Spirit is sovereign and obviously stirs things up, sometimes to near-fever pitch, and it is often rather difficult to tell which way the heavenly wind will carry us. He is quite unpredictable and reserves the right to turn things around, or upside-down, as He pleases. At such times, it seems the best we can do is seek to move with Him, but at the same time maintain a gracious and generous attitude toward all, even toward those who reject or malign us.

Jorge and I both knew that to maintain a sensitive ear to the Holy Spirit we had to be free of any sectarian attitude. And we knew too that if the awakening that we were seeing in the church in Argentina was to continue unchecked, it must not be confined to a denominational framework.

I remember telling Jorge that the time was upon us to be bold in declaring the unity of all of God's people. We discussed the matter quite seriously at night when we were alone after the meetings and on the train returning to Buenos Aires. It was quite clear to us that Jesus Christ was building one church, not a dozen or a thousand. We could see that his death destroyed the enmity between us and God, and therefore between us and our brothers in Christ. We knew that we were united in one Body. Yet we knew too that, practically speaking, we were fractured into many factions.

However, in our growing experience with the Gospel of the kingdom and the initial concepts of Christian discipleship, we had discovered an important principle: *Once a spiritual truth is seen, we must proclaim it in faith.* This in turn creates a consciousness of need and generates faith in the hearers. Then follows a period of discussion, enlightenment, struggle and adjustment. Finally, the new "wineskin" begins to emerge: a practical means of implementing the truth appears.

Consequently, I urged Jorge to study the whole question of the unity of the church as set forth in the Scriptures and then to bring a message on the subject in one of the Monday night meetings. He was a little reluctant at first, not because he had any doubts as to the scriptural basis or validity, but rather because he felt there might be some misunderstanding, and that some church leaders would imagine that we were declaring war on them. We figured others would think that we were trying to begin a new denomination. Such accusations were already being heard.

TWO TIMELY ARRIVALS

In the meantime, we had a pleasant surprise. A missionary in Paraguay with whom we had a close relationship, advised us that Arthur Wallis, a well-known author and conference-speaker from England, would soon be in South America. Immediately, we made arrangements to have him in Buenos Aires for some conferences and fellowship. Most of Wallis' ministry among us was based on the book of Nehemiah. As he spoke to us of spiritual renewal and reconstruction, emphasizing the need for integrity and a close walk with the Lord, we sensed the Lord was confirming to us the conditions necessary in order to rebuild the walls and define the proper outline of the city of God.

The partisan interests that had broken down relationships between different members of God's family were only serving to distract and delay the rebuilding of the original wall. As we pondered Nehemiah's specific task of assessing the situation, drawing up a work-plan and then coordinating the work on the wall between the many families, while defending the legitimacy of it all against outside attacks, our own situation began to take on new meaning.

A second event greatly encouraged us. Ever since Bentson and family had left Argentina in May, 1967, those who knew them continued to pray for their return. At last, in February, 1969, that longing became a reality.

Keith had completed his graduate course of

study and resigned from his mission. He sensed that he should cast his lot with the Christians in Buenos Aires, and work with the other pastors here on the closest possible terms. Since his visit to Argentina in October the previous year, he had kept in touch and was pretty well up-to-date on local developments. Thus he was able to move rather easily into the situation. After the initial "homecoming", it was almost as if he had never been away. Right away he was in the midst of all the activities and sharing the burden of ministry as "one of the fellows."

SECTARIAN SPIRIT BROKEN

Early in April the same year Jorge Himitian gave the first message in a Monday night meeting on the unity of all God's people. He pointed up the error in the traditional dichotomy: thinking of the church on one hand as a beautiful, mystical, ideal, heavenly entity in the mind of God; and on the other hand as a fractured, struggling, despised lot scattered over the earth. He told us that we must no longer separate Paul's epistles into 'doctrinal' and 'practical' portions in order to justify the distance separating these two facets in our own experience.

He dwelt especially upon Ephesians, chapter 4. There he underlined two realities that God has established and that we must recognize in practice: (1) that the legitimate conformation of the church includes the entire number of the redeemed in a city, and (2) that in the same area God has given to the church gifted ministries, all of which should be recognized by all the saints, and all of which should minister for the edification of the entire community.

This was illustrated in the Acts account of the church in Jerusalem, where *all* of the apostles ministered to *all* of the saints. Due in part to the vast size of the church there, community life was expressed on two levels (Acts 5:42; etc.): all together and from house to house (the latter, obviously, in small groups). The apostles did not divide the redeemed into twelve different groups, so that each could pastor a separate congregation. Rather, they maintained in practice the unity of the Spirit.

After giving the message, Jorge confided in me that he had some misgivings, not so much over the content, as over the timing. He wondered how the message was received and whether he had been too hasty or too forceful.

He need not have worried! The impact was tremendous. One after another approached us to say that it had broken the shackles on their minds. For the first time they had begun to think of themselves simply as Christians. And they began to see other Christians simply as brothers and sisters in the family of God.

It was as if all of us had unanimously decided to no longer take into account the denominational labels that anyone wore. Whether they were evident or not really didn't matter. Rather, it was a simple decision to recognize — from that time forward — that any and everyone who acknowledged Jesus Christ as Lord was part of our family.

In the following weeks, the consensus among the pastors was that the picture needed to be enlarged upon, and I was asked to bring further ministry on the subject. The series was titled "Moving Toward Unity," and — along with Jorge's message — was put into print with very little editing.

An interesting sidelight turned up when Jorge talked to me just after reviewing the transcript of his message for the printer. "I took out all the 'ifs' and the 'perhaps' and the rest of the conditional phrases," he said. In effect, when the message came out in print, it was more forceful and direct than the spoken word. The timing was clearly "right on".

One Monday night during the series "Moving Toward Unity," as Jorge was presiding over the meeting following the ministry from the Word, there was an intense time of prayer followed by a glorious sense of victory, which we interpreted as the breaking of sectarian chains in our minds. The truth is that since then the Lord has been moving us forward in constantly progressing steps toward unity, in spite of the problems that have appeared. This will be more thoroughly developed in a later chapter.

Perhaps an observation of Jorge most aptly illustrates the sense we had of what the Lord was doing in us at the time. Remembering Nehemiah's wall, he suggested that we should all labor in whatever place we found ourselves, but with a clear view of the ONE wall enclosing ALL the city. No longer should we work with a competitive or conflictive stance, but realize that we must all move toward a genuine and sincere manifestation of unity. It is God who is building us together; we are simply co-laborers with him.

TORTUGUITAS

In the northwestern suburbs of Buenos Aires, along National Highway No. 8 is a small semi-rural community bearing the name *TORTUGUITAS*, which in Spanish means "small turtles." It was here that the group of a dozen pastors from Greater Buenos Aires gathered for a never-to-be-forgotten week in August of the same year. We had concluded in our regular weekly sessions that we needed to retire somewhere for several days together to talk over the many things that were happening among us in the now rapidly expanding move of the Holy Spirit in our area.

Immediately following the Monday night meeting, we began gathering at a small restaurant just outside the city limits of the

Capital. Once all had arrived, we got into several cars and headed for Tortuguitas, where some friends had loaned us a weekend cottage in a quiet, somewhat isolated area. There we remained until Saturday afternoon without any specific program of activities and without any predefined hourly schedule for eating or rising or retiring. The days and the nights ran together in a very unconcerned fashion, as we gave ourselves wholeheartedly to intense discussion, devout worship and sincere heart-searching. We all felt the need to update our relationship and talk over our personal and coordinated responsibilities as we moved ahead together.

By Thursday afternoon whatever difficulties we had. with each other had basically been settled and we worshipped together in an absolutely free and uninhibited manner. There were tamborines, a trumpet, and an accordion. Those that were not playing an instrument used their own hands for clapping. We jumped, we sang, we laughed, we cried, we bowed in humble adoration, we repented, and we embraced. God was melting us together in order to use us in a closely coordinated manner for building up his people.

Then suddenly Keith disappeared from the circle that we had spontaneously formed as we prayed and worshipped in the living room. When he reappeared a few minutes later he had a towel draped over his left shoulder and a basin of water in his hands. Though most of those present had never seen anything like this, somehow we all knew instinctively that it was the right thing to do: we must wash each other's feet.

Keith knelt before one of the brothers and proceeded to remove his shoes and socks. This man was immediately moved to tears of humility and placed his hands on the head of this tall American who was already fervently praying for his brother while he washed his feet. The two were intently interceding for each other, as the rest of us gathered round in worship and thanksgiving. Everyone was waiting for his turn at the basin! So for nearly an hour we all had our opportunity to wash and get washed.

I shall never forget what happened when one of the pastors knelt before me to wash my feet. We both broke into sobs of love, humility and gratitude. Then suddenly I felt someone rubbing some liquid into my hair. When I looked up, I discovered that a third brother had gone into the bedroom and come back with a bottle of after-shave lotion which he was now applying to the top of my head!

Following this deeply emotional scene we all felt the need to give vent to our joy. We dashed into the large front yard where we ran and jumped, shouting praises to God. It looked like a scene from "The Sound of Music"!

Even when we didn't yet know all the consequences of the retreat, we all sensed a profound commitment to each other and to the Lord. He had set us free from our past and joined us together in love, faith, and confidence. The Lord knew how much we were in need of this binding together in order not to be dismayed over the mounting pressures opposing us.

9

FROM REVIVAL TO NORMALCY

"For the grace of God has appeared, bringing salvation to all men, instructing us to deny ungodliness and worldly desires and to live sensibly, righteously and godly in the present age."

— Titus 2:11, 12

The dozen or so pastors in Buenos Aires who were meeting regularly and bearing the principal responsibility for the large Monday night meetings were eminently churchmen. We all loved the church and were increasingly committed to the unity of the church. We have never seriously considered ourselves theologians in the more technical sense, but neither were we mystics. Our common interests and experiences had brought together a number of capable men who were already effective leaders. Yet hardly any could be properly classified as individualistic. That is to say, we had no interest in developing a "lone ranger" type mentality. From the beginning there has been consistently evident a concern for standing together and moving together.

I think it would be honest to say that our various gifts were manifest principally in preaching; especially this would have been true in the earlier years. We were articulators; although obviously some were more eloquent than others. Yet as we have grown together over the years, our intimacy and honesty have imposed upon us a greater priority: the need to be intensely practical. In a word, our search was for a very practical outworking of the Spirit-filled life.

Because of the new and dynamic dimension of

the Holy Spirit, different manifestations of a charismatic nature have been in evidence among us all along. Because of this, most visitors and outsiders have referred to us as a charismatic movement. As is usually the case (at least from the time of Paul's problem with the Corinthians), there have been spurious as well as genuine manifestations. In earlier chapters I referred to a couple dreams that served as "road signs" along the way. Speaking in tongues has been a common experience in prayer and worship, while with the accompanying gift of interpretation of tongues it has brought edification to the saints on different occasions. Prophetic utterance has been more in evidence in the meetings, but even so, not really in abundance.

Physical healings have also become a part of our experience, and many are the saints who have given testimony to such. Yet there has been no great emphasis on this particular aspect of ministry. This is not intended to be a defense or a justification; I am simply stating a fact.

Most of us have had effective results in the exorcising of evil spirits from demonized people seeking help. This facet of Christ's ministry has also been incorporated into the overall approach of the pastors in evangelism and the building of the church.

WARY OF THE SPURIOUS

While these and other charismatic manifestations have been and continue to remain in evidence, we have tended to shy away from practices which we felt were fanatical or disorderly. Our worship is generally uninhibited, but it is also orderly. Our singing and praise sometimes rise to high volumes, but the people recognize that a "sacred hush" is quite as valid. Tears of joy or of repentance frequently flow; singing is sometimes accompanied with rhythmic movements of the body; clapping and shouts of praise are often heard. Yet there is generally no sense of bondage to these more emotional experiences. The ebb and flow of such is accepted as normal.

There have been outbreaks of more spurious elements which have concerned us. One group, meeting in a suburban area without mature leadership, acquired an exaggerated view of the value of the prophetic gift. Through the supposed operation of this gift they were matching up the young people in couples, as well as determining the nature of their activities in church service and outreach.

In another case, in the interior of the country, a lady had a supposed angelic visitation. The angel then proceeded to inhabit her body and professed to be "one of the seven spirits of God," giving his name as "Valiant". Such extremes were not common nor were they widely known, but they were disturbing and gave a bad name to the spiritual renewal movement where they were known.

We were especially wary of anyone pretending to be "the voice" or "the prophet" of this fresh movement. Much blessing and encouragement had come to the saints through this heavenly awakening. It would be regrettable for the whole thing to be side-tracked.

Occasionally, some of the pastors among us would express a desire that we give a larger place to the charismatic element. They longed to see more of the supernatural. Such a concern was understandable, especially when many of them had just come out of a long, dry season in their life and ministry, and had experienced an initial touch of the power of God. For years they had been ham-strung by a tight and traditional ecclesiasticism that had explained away and justified the lack of the ineffable. Now that the fetters had fallen away and the mental bondage broken, they expected to find something more akin to "a miracle a day."

Our dilemma derived in part from the uncertainty of knowing how to achieve a larger supernatural element without encouraging the spurious. We had always enjoyed a remarkable liberty in worship and praise. But we had also observed that when we tended to go beyond the spontaneous, the strain to produce something introduced an unhealthy element into the picture. We also found that in a large and dynamic meeting, there were hardly ever lacking a few would-be prophets who were more than willing to oblige us and present us a show of their "supernatural" gifts. The results were invariably negative and disconcerting. Not entirely to the satisfaction of everyone, we concluded in a kind of pastoral concensus that we must simply continue to wait upon the Lord to handle things within his own time schedule. In the meantime, our responsibility was to seek always to be docile and sensitive to the Holy Spirit's leading.

PRAGMATIC OR MYSTICAL?

We realized that this openness to the Holy Spirit would only have meaning if we were engaged in the work that was clearly our major task: evangelizing, making disciples, edifying the Christian community until the believers were formed into a family of faithful, diligent saints. One of the things I insisted upon in conversations with the pastors was the need to concentrate on building the congregations on the basis of families. For some time I had been uneasy about the common viewpoint of so many pastors and missionaries who see the youth as almost the only promising candidates for developing leaders.

I was convinced we needed to give more time to men, heads of families. Certainly it was a more painstaking procedure, but it was the only way to establish families. I saw that if we concentrated on family-life, then the formation of the children and young people — and even the formation of new Christians — would be a simpler task. This proved to be one of the more significant decisions that we made together in the process of spiritual renewal. Over the years, more and more emphasis has been placed upon the family unit, which is the basic unit of society as well as the church, so that our various congregations have become strongly family-oriented.

At the same time Keith and Juan Carlos were becoming especially articulate in insisting upon the conviction that was growing in all of us, that instead of seeking revival, our principal concern should be to seek normalcy. God was interested in redeeming us in order to normalize our lives.

In his first general epistle Peter indicates that we have been redeemed from a vain, useless way of life (1:18). Elsewhere in the same letter he says that our behavior — way of life — should be holy, excellent, chaste and respectful (1:15, 2:12, 3:1, 2). Salvation then, in very practical terms, ought to initiate a basic change in our behavior, or way of life.

Often Keith would ask the question, "Why did God create men on the earth?" Then he would give the answer: "In order to live a wholesome, normal life, to work, to serve others, to raise a family." If this was God's will and order in creation, then redemption should restore us to effective and fruitful living in these areas. Moreover — Keith pointed out — Paul told Titus in the second chapter of his letter that "sound doctrine" involved being temperate, dignified, sensible . . . reverent, not gossips, not enslaved to wine, workers at home, denying ungodliness and living sensibly, righteously and godly in the present age. The entire scope of this "sound doctrine" sounds very down-to-earth and matter-of-fact, and not very "spiritual" to a religious mentality. Yet Paul wound up the chapter telling Titus that these things were to be spoken with all authority!

By the end of 1969 it was becoming eminently clear to us that the Holy Spirit was telling us to seek a return to normal, and not simply a "revival". Our conviction was that we must concentrate on being the men, the women, the parents, the wives and husbands, the employees, the professionals, the citizens that God made us to be, both in creation and in redemption. Then, if he deigns to do something more, something special, something remarkable, that's his prerogative. We were discovering that the pragmatic side of things was our principal responsibility; on the mystical side of the ledger, we could only remain open to God and "abide in Him" in the daily exercise of faith and obedience, without strain or hurry.

In October of that year Jorge Himitian preached a moving message at a pastoral retreat in Chaco province, entitled "SAVE SOULS OR SAVE MEN?" After presenting the problem of sin evidenced in the distortion of human life, and the deficient Gospel of the evangelical who seeks only the salvation of souls, Jorge bore down on the validity of God's answer: the Gospel of God's government which completely reorients the life and behavior of the true disciple of Christ, and brings together a community of saints who live and work with integrity, who show the love, the grace and the truth of God in everyday living.

YEAR'S END IN SOLDINI

The last week of the year, between Christmas and Jan. 1, 1970, twenty-odd pastors, including a number from the interior of the country as well as from Buenos Aires, gathered for a spiritual retreat in a Christian camp in Soldini, just outside the city of Rosario. Perhaps the largest issue in focus there was the nature of our relationships with each other, and how we could most effectively implement the restructuring of our congregations in accord with the scriptural teaching concerning discipleship. But underlying the entire retreat was the larger philosophical and theological issue of mysticism versus pragmatism. One or another of the pastors showed some discontent with the more pragmatic posture that the majority had adopted. The difference of focus was quite clear in an encounter we had the middle of the week.

One of the pastors had been involved in a significant spiritual awakening which began some two decades earlier, and which had been born along for a time through some spectacular and supernatural elements, with healings playing a prominent role. His real desire was that we would relate to that earlier outpouring and see that our own experience was principally the fruit of that awakening and the ensuing intercession. But this we could not honestly do, and our reluctance bothered him.

On the afternoon in question, as we sat under the trees together, we listened to his exposition on the love of God, a beautiful message that left us all deeply touched over the greatness of God. A discussion followed, in which several expressed their gratitude for the ministry just concluded, while revealing their concern for the brother's apparent aloofness and seeming disdain toward the rest of us. At that point, he said to us, "Your problem is that you think that this movement of the Holy Spirit began two years ago, when in reality it began twenty years ago."

To which one of the pastors responded, "No, brother, not two years ago, nor twenty years ago . . . it began two thousand years ago."

We have a saying in Argentina which aptly describes his reaction: "He put his violin in its case, and took off." He seemed sure that was the end of "the movement"!

10

TIGHTENING THE JOINTS

"The entire body, being supplied and held together by the joints and ligaments, grows with a growth which is from God."

— Colossians 2:19b

The summer sky was studded with stars as we sat together on the lawn in Soldini to see the old year out and the new one in. More than a score of pastors had gathered from strategic points around the country to pray and talk together. We reviewed the steps through which the Lord had led us up to that point. Even with the opposition from traditionalists within various denominations, interest was growing around the country. The mutual commitment among the pastors seemed firm and our goals were becoming clearer. We felt we had a solid scriptural basis for our proclamation of the Gospel of God's government and the unity of the church. The general lines of our varied and complementary ministries were now more clearly defined. I remember that as we shared together those final hours of 1969, we expressed our expectation that 1970 would be a "year of glory."

Looking back on it now, it is clear that our anticipation was rather naive and pretentious. Serious adjustments had yet to be made and, above all, everything had to be put to the test. We had hardly stopped to realize that we had made considerable advance in our thinking, but many of the traditional church structures continued just as before. Some of them were beginning to groan under the pressure of the fermenting new wine.

CLOCK-WATCHERS DON'T WORSHIP

True, a number of changes had been made, two of which were especially obvious: the time and importance given to worship, and the format of the meeting place. Clearly, Jesus Christ was the Center and the Head of the church; therefore, our shift towards a strong and vital place for worship was logical and valid. No longer did we view the 'song service' as simply a psychological preparation of the audience to hear the preaching of the Word of God. Nor did we feel the need for the worship to be strictly programmed and directed by a special song-leader. We discovered that when believers are filled with the Holy Spirit they're normally 'bubbling over' with a desire to praise and express their love and gratitude to the Lord. So our meetings had become quite spontaneous times of open and free worship.

There was little need to "prime the pump"; hence the leader was more a coordinator than a director. And whereas newcomers occasionally had some initial difficulty understanding the differences between our meetings and others of a more traditional nature, as a rule they were soon caught up in the love, the joy, the spontaneous fervor of saints that were more than willing to share their experience of Christ.

Since the early meetings in the Darling home we determined not to be enslaved by the clock. Worship requires an unhurried drawing near to the Throne of grace, a sensitive openness to the gentle breeze of the Holy Spirit, a broad participation of the worshippers. This takes time. Clock-watchers don't worship. Even to this date, a typical time of worship in our meetings will run from forty-five minutes to an hour-and-a-half. Quite a departure from the "three songs and a prayer with one special number" of yester-year!

INFORMAL ARRANGEMENTS

The change in seating arrangements seemed to happen without much planning. Probably due in part to the living room atmosphere of the early meetings, the leaders and people alike realized that an arrangement that permitted us to look each other in the face occasionally, was conducive to worship, testimony and wider participation. One brother expressed it succinctly several years ago when he said, "It's hard to worship when all you see is the back of other people's heads!" What a difference when radiant faces are everywhere to be seen!

In the typical church auditoriums where the congregations were experiencing this transforming process, the pastor often opted for a removal of the pulpit from the podium. Either the same pulpit or a small table to replace it was then set up toward the side of the hall, on the floor level with the rest of the congregation. Then the benches or chairs were rearranged in such fashion that as many as possble were facing the center of the hall. We sought an arrangement that was informal and flexible.

I should underline the fact that these changes were incorporated NOT to bring about a renewal, but were the direct result of an increase in worship and a desire to get Christ back into the center of things. It was as though there was a general feeling that man had occupied center-stage long enough!

We also tended to draw away from the idea that a special building was necessary. We felt no need for a special religious atmosphere to be created by architecture or interior decorations. As a matter of fact, many felt that such things were more a burden or "drag" on us than a help. Gradually, we were turning away from something static to a more dynamic approach to worship. Buildings were not especially attractive to us; we felt God was more interested in forming a "people", a temple made of living stones.

Our shift in the ensuing years to a greater emphasis on home gatherings, open air meetings, and special conferences held in gymnasiums was a logical outgrowth of those concerns. Essentially, we were learning to feel quite at home in whatever atmosphere or situation; it was the gathering body of joyful believers that "set the stage" and determined the atmosphere.

Within this context there was a growing respect for the value of a heavenly anointing on those who ministered the Word, or exercised some spiritual gift, or even on those that prayed or gave a word of testimony. We found this was more important than a merely intellectual preparation. This was not a disdain for the intellectual; it rather grew out of a conviction that something more, something divine, something ineffable, should characterize the service and the preaching of the servants of the Lord.

One of the major factors underlying these changes and making them feasible was the strong mutual commitment, the unity and cooperation, that existed among the group of pastors. There is little doubt that many would have been reluctant to make these changes and shifts in emphasis and context, had they been moving alone, or had they found stiff resistance from their most intimate colleagues. But together we found strength and confidence; together we were able to withstand the tides of opposition from without; together we were able to avoid the more obvious mistakes; together we were willing to experiment.

BONE TO BONE

Still, we were acutely aware that these

structural changes had to do mainly with externals. More vital to us were questions relating to life-style, service and relationships. Late in 1969 we had been impressed with Paul's use of the words "joints" and "ligaments" as analogies of the spiritual relationships which exist between people in the Body of Christ (see Ephes. 4:16 and Colos. 2:19). This indicated a greater intimacy and mutual dependence than we had previously known.

As we thought and talked more about it, we realized that, just as the joints in the human body give it flexibility, strength, nourishment, and coordination, so would a closer relationship between the saints provide these same qualities. We felt too, that Ezekiel's vision and prophecy over the dry bones was a timely word for us. As the Spirit swept over the piles of bones, we are told that the bones came together, bone to its bone. With further prophecy, they were fleshed out and "stood on their feet, an exceedingly great army." We concluded that it was vain to think we would ever see the church as a mighty army unless the saints came to have a more vital relationship between them, every "bone to its bone."

By this time, most of us were involved in the transition from traditional evangelistic methods to obedience to Christ's command to make disciples. We were understanding increasingly the need to concentrate on forming lives, shaping character, building a life-style, attitudes and outlook that honored the Lord.

When a newcomer turned to the Lord, one of the saints would take specific responsibility for him, begin visiting him at home, winning his confidence, praying with him. Major areas of his life would be exposed to the teaching of Christ and the apostles; this would invariably include family relationships, job situations and attitudes, handling of money and integration into the Christian community. Prayer, Bible reading and witnessing were no longer isolated "spiritual" areas; they were vitally related to every other area of day-to-day living.

Early experiences of this kind awakened in the pastors the consciousness of a need for some training sessions to be provided for the believers who were making this transition. We became aware that the Monday night meetings were not ideally geared to meet this need. By now, we were getting accustomed to changes. Change had almost become the order of the day!

In October of the previous year, we had already shifted from the overcrowded hall on Catamarca street to a nearby movie theater. With a seating capacity of over a thousand, we had room for expansion. But on occasion, it too was jammed.

DOERS, AND NOT HEARERS ONLY

Even so, a disenchantment with the big meetings was setting in. More and more people were coming out of a desire to see and feel something spectacular. The appetites of some were becoming a bit jaded, and many were not really interested in making the changes that God seemed to be requiring of us. Still, a majority — mostly those who had been following these developments closely over the past year or two — were vitally interested in going on, in growing, in moving toward maturity. They had been delivered from sectarianism and had seriously committed themselves to Christ and to his people. Having been instrumental in bringing them this far, we felt a keen responsibility to keep moving ahead in God's unfolding program of spiritual renewal.

One step was taken in this direction when the group of pastors whose congregations were located within the capital city of Buenos Aires decided to start a training course with the principal people of their communities. In June

(1970) a group first numbering two or three hundred began meeting on Saturday nights at the hall on Hidalgo street. This involved Keith Bentson, Juan Carlos Ortiz, Jorge Himitian, and Augusto Ericsson, all of whom shared in the ministry. By now, several of us were making serious moves toward merging with each other, so as to unite our congregations under a plurality of pastors. The Saturday training session was a tentative move in that direction, partly to consider the feasibility of further steps toward merger.

Those Saturday night meetings were divided into two periods of teaching. Basically, it was instruction on how to disciple new believers: determining a Christian life-style, fixing goals, suggesting practical steps. Also dealt with were ways to establish close, working relationships between the saints in a congregation.

Juan Carlos, Jorge, and Ivan had already been working on the problem of getting their own groups reorganized. They were trying to get their people free from the "Sunday church-goer" mentality. They wanted them to become participators in the process of spiritual edification, and not merely spectators. James refers to this need in his general epistle when he says we should be "doers of the word, and not merely hearers" (James 1:22).

The ways these relationships were developed varied from one congregation to another. But the procedure Ortiz used was typical. First he selected, after prayer for the Holy Spirit's guidance, a group of men which he proposed to train for leadership in the church. He started spending time with them each week individually and together as a group. The first goal was simply to get well acquainted and touch the spiritual "heartbeat" of each one. He wanted to bring together a tightly-related and firmly committed team of men who would bear the burden of responsibilities mutually.

Then after several months, through discussion and prayer, each of these men began to single out in a similar way other members of the congregation, with a view toward relating them more directly to himself as their immediate shepherd or counsellor, as a kind of spiritual mentor. As each small nucleus, or cell group, was being formed they began meeting once a week in the home of the leader. Ortiz in turn was developing courses of study to use in his training sessions with these leaders. As these were mimeographed and later printed, the leaders themselves started using this material to teach those under their care. The nearly constant flow of fresh material, plus the large Monday night meetings and the Saturday teaching sessions, provided an abundance of material that at times was even difficult for the pastors to keep abreast of.

"THE MOVEMENT IS DEAD"

Obviously, we were becoming more pragmatic in our approach to church renewal, and getting more involved in working out the details of relationships between the believers, so as to put together a valid structure for evangelism, discipleship and building up of the people of God. At the same time, we were hearing accusations to the effect that we were losing interest in the more charismatic element, which had earlier been in greater prominence.

So now, apart from the opposition from the more traditional elements in the church who felt we were too radical, we were getting static from the more "charismatic" elements who said we were not radical enough! Word began to spread that "the movement is dead."

As we talked it over among the pastors, two things seemed clear. First, it was pointless to try to defend ourselves. This had not been our style up to now; and besides, the whole thing we were doing seemed so new and unproven to outsiders that, in any case, we had little evidence to present in our favor. Second, we felt we must not allow ourselves to be distracted with subjective issues. The Lord, we felt, had set before us some specific objectives and we must get on with the task at hand.

At this point we made an important decision. It looked like a retreat to many, but for those of us involved in the process since the beginning, it was a significant tactical step. We decided to suspend the Monday night gatherings. We felt they had fulfilled the purpose for which they had existed. If they outlived their usefulness they could become abortive to the whole process.

These meetings had been especially used to restore vital worship among the Christians in Buenos Aires. Whereas when they began there was hardly any other group or meeting that gave such priority to worship, now there were congregations in many different parts of the city and surrounding suburbs whose worship was vital and rich. In some places it was a Baptist church, in others it was the Christian and Missionary Alliance; elsewhere it was the Plymouth Brethren or an undenominational group. The spiritual awakening was spreading rapidly throughout all the various denominations in Argentina, and many of the leaders were experiencing the fulness of the Holy Spirit.

Another purpose had been clearly achieved. These meetings had served to bring together church leaders and people from many different backgrounds who were now firmly committed to each other and to the unity of the Body of Christ. These would never be the same. God was tightening the joints between us. We were finding a growing satisfaction with being simply the people of God. As a matter of fact, we were so occupied with what was happening among us and in our more immediate surroundings, that we were not aware that many others were watching and waiting at a distance.

Yet the news was getting out. And where it went it found receptive ears and hearts. In April, World Vision, Inc. had sponsored a national pastors' conference in Argentina. Dr. Paul Rees, in charge of the planning, had suggested to Dr. Luis Bacafusco of the Argentine Federation of Evangelical Churches that one of the speakers on the program should be an Argentine. Right away, Bucafusco mentioned the name of Juan Carlos Ortiz.

As it turned out, Juan Carlos was the evening speaker and his subject was church renewal and evangelism. Every evening he challenged more than seven hundred pastors and church leaders to make room in their lives and in their church structures for the mighty moving of the Spirit of God, as he exercises and implements the Lordship of Christ throughout the earth. The final night he delivered an eloquent address on the unity of the church, based on the unity of Christ himself, and prophesied that God would bring together His people in all the earth. It was a bold statement, but it went home to many hearts. Henceforth, a broad spectrum of Christian leaders could not deny that something new and dynamic — perhaps radical, but certainly impossible to ignore — was coming into shape on the horizon. Those who were hoping for the curtain to be drawn on the performance were yet to discover that it had only just begun!

11

RUN WITH THE VISION

"Record the vision and inscribe it on tablets, that the one who reads it may run. For the vision is yet for the appointed time; it hastens toward the goal and it will not fail."

— Habakkuk 2:2, 3

While there was obviously yet much to learn and much to do, we had seen enough to know that God had gotten hold of us with a revolutionary vision. For four years He had been "putting us through the paces" and we had been endeavoring to do our homework diligently. The few contacts we had established with others both in the Argentine interior and outside the country had been quite encouraging, in the sense that we found real openness to what we shared. The preaching of the Gospel of God's government and the proclamation of Christ's lordship was arousing interest in many places. Our own congregations were doing well and growing, learning the first steps of Christian discipleship and seeing the fruit of obedience to God.

The next couple years we greatly expanded our contacts with other countries. We also had a number of visitors from the U.S.A., Central and South America, all of whom made valuable contributions and extended our spiritual horizons. Costa Rica, Panama, Colombia, Ecuador and other countries were visited by several of us from Buenos Aires, and warm personal relationships were developing between us, as the Spirit of God was sweeping over one country after another.

In March, 1972, we had what turned out to be our first Latin American spiritual retreat with church leaders attending from nearly a dozen different nations. As we worked on the agenda for ministry the feeling among the pastors here was that we should focus on the nature of the church in three facets: as a people, as a temple, and as a body. Keith developed the thought of the church as a people, a community, a holy nation, having a single identity and a common life. He emphasized the practical side of spiritual life in the home, on the job, in everyday living out the life of Christ in us.

I presented the church as the temple of God, the place of His presence in the earth. Here we saw the meaning of worship, holiness and communion. Together we considered God's pleasure in His people and our call to reflect His glory and grace.

Jorge developed the theme of relationships within the Body of Christ, our vital union with Christ and with each other. He spoke of the joints and the spiritual nourishment that flows between the members when this relationship is properly evaluated.

Different brothers shared in leading the meetings which abounded in worship and glad celebration. The testimonies and ministry from brothers of other countries was most appreciated. It was indeed a glorious experience for us all to learn of the sovereign ways that the Lord was moving among His people in so many disparate places throughout Latin America.

FARTHER AFIELD

In the middle of the year nine pastors from Argentina, mostly from our group in Buenos Aires, were invited to Chile to cooperate with an equal number of Chilean ministers during a three-week period of ministry planned by Evangelism in Depth. It was called "Operation Forty" since it was geared to reach forty cities and towns in southern Chile. There we ministered among Baptists, Christian and

Missionary Alliance, Anglicans and various Pentecostal groups, winding up all together in the city of Temuco for three very intensive days of meetings. The final night Juan Carlos ministered to a packed house in the city's largest Baptist church. In the midst of Chile's political and social turmoil it was indeed a bright and refreshing time.

1973 was also a time of great blessing and expansion. In May, we had a large five-day retreat in the government hotel complex at Embalse Río Tercero, in the province of Córdoba. Busloads of Christians came from Brazil, Paraguay, and Chile, as well as from many distant places within Argentina. Immediately following that, Augusto Ericsson and I were invited to England for six weeks of ministry. In August, Juan Carlos went through several Latin American countries, winding up with an extensive time of ministry in the U.S. In November, Keith and I were invited to the Philadelphia/Delaware Valley area for three weeks of conferences, including a significant four-day retreat in New Jersey, which brought together many leaders from around the U.S. and Canada.

IN THE ARGENTINE INTERIOR

Closer to home we were seeing encouraging fruits of church renewal in various cities in the interior of Argentina. In the far northwest Juvenal García had recently graduated from the Baptist seminary in Buenos Aires where he had been filled with the Holy Spirit. He was doing a fine job leading his home church forward in the northwest province of Jujuy. The Lord poured out His blessing upon the saints there and they have since been growing and expanding their ministry throughout the province.

Down in Santa Rosa, capital city of La Pampa province, the Baptists and the Mennonites got together and the Lord poured out his Holy Spirit upon both the pastors and their wives and many of the leading saints in both congregations. This brought quite a commotion to the Mennonites in other parts of Argentina, many of whom were subsequently filled with the Spirit.

Rosario, a city of a million people in Santa Fe province, has for years had a thriving congregation which began under the ministry of a retired railroad-man. He was for many years an able preacher among the Brethren assemblies until he was disfellowshipped in 1967 because of his charismatic experience with the Holy Spirit. A few young people started meeting in his home, later filling the garage, and then overflowing a rented hall. They, too, have expanded their ministry to many neighboring towns, while maintaining an active evangelistic witness in the central plaza and in the halls of the local university.

These are typical situations. In smaller towns as well as in large cities around the country, God is stirring the hearts of His people. And as they experience renewal and refreshing, they move out in effective witness to those around them who need the Gospel. Vast responsibilities lie before us, but the heavenly flame is burning in many hearts throughout the land. Our hopes are high as we look out over the horizon.

LESSONS GLEANED

As already indicated, a number of the pastors from Buenos Aires have traveled extensively throughout the country, ministering especially on the recurring themes of the Gospel of the kingdom, Christian discipleship, the fulness of the Holy Spirit, the unity of the church, worship, etc. Books, pamphlets, Bible study outlines, and cassettes have been published and distributed widely. Certainly, no one can say that "this thing was done in a corner."

It will not come as a surprise to my readers to

learn, however, that a glorious beginning is no guarantee of continued blessing. Sometimes we have been quite distressed to see a city, where a few months earlier the pastors and saints were flowing together in joy, love and unity, later divided again into factions and seemingly unable to maintain the "unity of the Spirit." On occasion we have been able to help the brethren resolve their differences, but at other times all our efforts have been to no avail.

Through all these experiences, both positive and negative, certain principles seem to be indicated as essential if the uniting of the Christians who have experienced a spiritual renewal is to continue unchecked. Let me suggest a few, without pretending to be all-encompassing:

1) There must be able leadership, men with large hearts and clear goals. Small-minded men seem incapable of the flexibility and tolerance needed as the church goes through adjustments and changes, developing new relationships and learning to walk in the Spirit. If there is self-seeking or an overweening concern for personal advantage, a monkey-wrench is thrown into the gear-box that will hinder or even completely negate the gentle movings of the Holy Spirit to bring together God's people.

2) It is necessary to develop a docility or sensitivity to the Holy Spirit, and not fall into the enemy's trap of breaking the harness and dashing forward with some extreme proposition. Much patience is required, both in dealing with others and in regards to our own ideals and illusions. If we impetuously rush headlong into whatever occurs to us, we risk destroying valuable relationships and even grieving the Holy Spirit.

3) As one brother stated it, we are learning to be relationship-oriented, rather than project-oriented. We are no longer as concerned with "getting a job done" as we are with learning to

walk together in God's grace. This matter of relationships has become a high priority for the exercise of our faith. We sincerely believe it is not God's will for His servants to walk alone. Every man of God should concentrate on nurturing and maintaining warm and confident relationships with other men of God. By this we imply more than simply a fraternal appreciation. We must learn to take correction, respond to exhortations, encourage each other and intercede for each other.

THE NEED FOR COMPANIONSHIP

In watching the development of spiritual renewal and church unity in different areas, we have observed that two kinds of situations seem to offer the greatest hope for continuance. If, in a given city, a group of pastors will clearly commit themselves to stand together, get intimately acquainted, open their lives to each other, make adjustments so as to walk together, determine not to push each other but to depend upon gentle persuasion and the power of the Holy Spirit, then a whole new picture of the church begins to unfold. It is absolutely necessary to understand that this will take time — months, and even years — to develop. But to reach a position of mutual commitment and confidence, where love and loyalty to each other underlie the relationships, is more than worth all the effort and sacrifice.

To illustrate such a situation, I could mention briefly what is happening in Quito, Ecuador. A group of four or five pastors working in different parts of the city manifested such a hunger for walking together in the Spirit that they threw their fears to the wind and opened up to the breeze of the Holy Spirit. Jorge Himitian was with them for a weekend retreat when they all broke before the Lord and got a lot of things out in the open, making room for God to work deeply in their lives. They have since gone through some severe testing times, but they are growing, evangelizing, working in many homes and making an increasing impact upon their city. Clearly, they have no interest in returning to the former state of things where each one worked in his own corner and did things his own way.

Oftentimes, however, such intimacy and confidence seem most difficult to obtain locally. A pastor may find that no other pastors close to him are willing or ready for such a transparent walk with another brother. In that case, he will be wise to seek such a relationship with others that are moving in this way, even if they are distant. He should seek to relate closely with one or more who are already walking together in such unity. This will greatly facilitate his own progress and reorientation.

As an example of this kind of situation, several of us are providing oversight and intimate comradeship for various pastors in the area surrounding our city (within a few hours by car or bus), and, in a slightly looser relationship, with others who are further afield. This consists of frequent personal contact and counseling, providing them with specific orientation as to how to handle different situations, improving their relationship with their own congregations and generally seeking to enhance their fruitfulness and their walk in victory and joy.

AMONG THE CATHOLICS

In concluding this chapter I should make at least a passing reference to our developing friendship with some Roman Catholic priests. Since 1969 we have had a warm relationship with Alberto Ibanez Padilla, a Jesuit who was the first priest in Argentina to experience the baptism in the Holy Spirit. Angel Negro and I spent several days with him in a Trappist monastery in 1970, where God was pouring out His spirit upon the monks. Shortly thereafter, Keith, Jorge, and I were invited by Alberto to an Easter retreat where the four of us ministered together and several Catholic laypeople were filled.

About that time, Juan Carlos was invited to Montevideo, Uruguay, by a priest who had recently been filled when he prayed for him. The priest wanted Juan Carlos to preach the Gospel to his people and pray for them to be filled with the Holy Spirit. The results far exceeded what anyone expected. Even the bishop sent a personal emissary to check things out! Fortunately, he returned to give a good report!

The present leader of the Catholic charismatics in Argentina is a gracious priest of Spanish origin: Francisco Muñoz. The movement is spreading throughout the country, even though there is some resistance from ecclesiastical authorities in several areas. Many priests, nuns, and laypeople have been filled with the Spirit and have found a new joy and release to share Christ with others. They have many dynamic prayer groups scattered over the city of Buenos Aires.

We have also had a growing fellowship with several priests that work with the "Focolares" movement, originating in Italy during the Second World War. This lively group, which emphasizes fraternity and community and has a rather ecumenical stance, seems very warm and open to the work of the Spirit of God.

Obviously, any spiritual movement in Latin America, if it is to be extensive, must involve the Roman Catholics. Therefore, it should not be surprising to us to see the Lord sovereignly stirring hearts and revealing Himself in grace and goodness to the many sincere seekers and worshippers among them. We believe that what He has begun, He will also bring to maturity. Our testimony and confidence is that Jesus Christ is building His church around the world wherever

He finds open hearts, and we rejoice in that glad reality.

12

MATURING THROUGH CONFLICTS

"Iron sharpens iron, so one man sharpens another."

— Proverbs 27:17

A saintly, snow-haired man of God gave me a word of wisdom years ago: "Everything that is of God will be tested . . . yet everything that is of God will stand the test." Time and again, as I've found things shaking around me — and sometimes within me — I've recalled those words. And I've mused over the fact that you never really know how firm a foundation anything has until it is shaken. For that reason, early appraisals or hasty conclusions often prove erroneous. One has to patiently await the testing which reveals the validity as well as the weakness of whatever is put to the test.

In retrospect it now seems quite logical and clear that our discoveries and our works had to undergo testing. Our relationships had to be tested; our theories and ideas had to be shaken; our integrity had to be tested. In reality, we have been shaken and sifted a number of times. Clearly, we can never say that the testing has come to an end. Yet out of it all, once the dust has settled and careful appraisal is made, we have found that the trial has been basically salutary. In the process, patience and maturity seem to be built into the lives of those who lean heavily upon the Lord. Human enthusiasm tends to take a back seat, and advance is made on the basis of the grace of God and simple obedience.

How nice it would be to say that our story of church renewal has all been a matter of love, grace and glory! But it would be both unrealistic and dishonest. We have had our problems, temptations, defeats, and losses.

In the beginning, since the majority of us came from non-pentecostal church backgrounds, we were accused of turning Pentecostal for having experienced the baptism in the Holy Spirit and the manifestation of spiritual gifts such as prophecy and tongues. Others, more daring, classed us with the Spiritists, and accused us of having introduced "spiritistic" elements into our worship.

Many of the Pentecostals, in the earlier days of the Spirit's outpouring among us, delightfully anticipated that our experience would bring an increase in their ranks, especially since they knew that several had been disfellowshipped from their congregations. When this did not materialize, some turned on us saying that we were out to form a new denomination.

With the passing of the first couple years, we became very aware of the fact that what we were experiencing was more than a charismatic movement. Rather, the Lord was involving us in His own larger purpose of spiritual restoration of the church. Through the work of the Holy Spirit, God began to restore many long-forgotten truths (for us, at least) from His Word such truths as: recognition of the lordship of Christ as an essential condition for salvation, the Gospel of the kingdom of God, discipleship, the unity of the church, etc. Moreover, we had to make many adjustments in our concepts concerning repentance, baptism, the Lord's table, the operation of spiritual gifts and ministries, meeting halls, pastoral care, etc. All this exposed us to a new charge: 'false doctrine' and 'heresy'.

Because of our emphasis on the unity of the church, we were derogatorily classified as "ecumenical". And for our contacts with the Roman Catholics, we were judged as taking part in the "great whore" of the Apocalypse.

In the measure that some of our congregations started taking positive steps toward merger and unity, we heard accusations to the effect that we were 'power-hungry', ambitious, and wanting to form some kind of 'super-church'. In spite of these charges, our congregations, retreats and united meetings continued to manifest a spiritual dynamic and enthusiasm that often attracted believers from other groups. This facet earned us another epithet: 'sheep-stealers'. And I've already referred to conflicts we had with some over an exaggerated tendency toward mysticism.

However, except for these passing references, I don't think it worthwhile to labor over such incidents. In any case, they were short-lived and hardly worthy of serious consideration. The distress caused by the false accusations was only momentary, whereas the conviction that God was with us remained firm.

These peripheral problems probably served even more to clarify our vision and to draw us closer one to another. We were growing in conviction and in our relationship with each other. The Gospel was being proclaimed with a clear clarion voice; we were becoming more adept at forming the lives and shaping the attitudes of the newly converted. We felt secure in our vision of the lordship of Christ, encouraged in our conviction that it was possible to live together according to the nature of the church, ministering according to the gifts and graces that God gives, all in an atmosphere of love and mutual submission. There was simplicity and confidence in our commitment to each other.

DISCORD

Yet, in all these years, the most serious conflict that we had to face was not with other groups of Christians, but with one of our own colleagues. Basically, the problem arose over a situation which could be presented in the form of a question: How should we proceed with a pastor who has been found living covertly in sexual immorality? If, when confronted, he humbles himself and repents, can he continue exercising his ministry, without interruption? Can a pastor who has been deceiving his congregation, living in immorality, continue to preach and teach others to live righteously, immediately following his act of repentance? (This was not for us simply a hypothetical problem; rather, we had to face just such a situation).

For the entire group of pastors — with one exception — there was no doubt in our minds that such a fault in the conduct of a servant of God would disqualify him, at least for a time, from continuing to exercise pastoral ministry. But one of our colleagues differed strongly with us. And therein lay our conflict.

Our brother alleged that he had received a new understanding about the nature of forgiveness through a friend in another country. His position was based on the following argument: "When a brother, who has been living in sin, sincerely repents, no matter how grave his faults, the blood of Christ cleanses him from all sin, and God in His great love promises to never again remember his sins against him. Therefore, we ought to do the same. And if we don't remember his sins against him, then we have no reason to disqualify him from the ministry."

We were in complete agreement with our brother concerning the concept of God's forgiveness and pardon of past sins that have been confessed and abandoned. What we found inadmissible was his contention that forgiveness was equivalent to an immediate restitution to the ministry. Moreover, we were really alarmed at our brother's unwillingness to modify his position. On the one hand, it caused us serious concern that he should determine unilaterally what should be done, rejecting the consensus of all the remaining pastors. And on the other, we foresaw with great preoccupation what confusion and laxity might be created in the churches, if pastors and Christian leaders, discovered in adultery or fornication, could continue ministering on the sole condition of a statement of repentance.

It seemed clear to us that God's forgiveness of a sinner establishes fellowship with God and with the saints. But to bear an office of spiritual responsibility in the church, according to the clear teaching of the Word of God, certainly requires more than simple forgiveness. The apostle Paul points out that an overseer (bishop, pastor, elder) must be "above reproach," an example to the flock. This is an essential condition for pastoral ministry. It is not principally his eloquence that makes a pastor "apt to teach," but rather his life and exemplary conduct. Once his transgression has been forgiven, he is to be included in the fellowship of the church, but if a man's life has not been exemplary, in the period immediately following his forgiveness he has no moral authority to teach others.

Moreover, Paul says that to be qualified as a bishop or pastor, the man "must have a good reputation with those outside the church" (I Tim. 2:27). A "good reputation" is not acquired from one day to the next. It is the result of a consistent testimony over a period of time of righteousness and honorable conduct.

After serious and lengthy consideration of the question, all the remaining pastors (except one who was uncertain what position to take) expressed to our colleague the conviction that the brother in the condition mentioned above should be relieved of all ministerial responsibility and should refrain from any further pastoral responsibility until the church, through its leaders, lifts the disciplinary measure, on consideration of a reputable testimony over a reasonable period of time. In the meantime, having heard his confession, the church should receive him into fellowship. During this time of restraint from ministry, the brother should give diligence to be a good Christian disciple, and seek a complete restoration of both his personal and family life.

Our insistence on dealing with the matter in this way only served to entrench our colleague in his former position. Personally, he had already forgiven and restored the brother to ministry, and was unwilling to review his decision with us.

SOME VALUABLE LESSONS LEARNED

I believe it is fair to say that nothing in all these years together has caused us more distress and heart searching than this matter. Yet in truth it did not cause us to harbor resentments or judgmental attitudes. To the contrary, in spite of the very painful process, throughout the duration of the problem there was evident a sincere attitude of love and patience, as well as a deep desire on the part of all to see all the barriers overcome and the healing process completed. Finally, we got through and reconciliation was effected. But during the time of conflict we were forced to extensively examine our motivations and our moral principles, and not simply review the events and the consequences. Besides what has been said above, perhaps it would be helpful to mention some of the more important lessons we learned.

First of all, in the midst of our struggle, we had to stabilize ourselves before the eloquent arguments presented us concerning the efficacy of love. In point of fact, this spiritual renewal in Argentina, as in many parts of the world, has been characterized by deep, sincere love. It has changed for the better our proclamation of the Gospel; it has healed families and ordered and adjusted our relationships within the Christian community. You should see how these Argentines hug one another! And now, being faced with the moral collapse of a dear man with a beautiful family, who would not be moved with deep compassion? Our own colleague was an example to us also. He loved this man and wanted to save him at all costs.

Our conflict, however, soon became an issue of love vs. righteousness. We considered it right and correct that amends be made in the proper fashion, because of the conviction that only on the basis of such right action can there ever be a wholesome and lasting healing. When one or another of the pastors would venture to persuade our colleague of his need to reconsider his position, the response would almost invariably be a defense based on an "all-encompassing love" that forgives and forgets without requiring any further clarification. Superficially, it would seem that a love that forgives and immediately restores to the ministry would be greater than a love that disciplines and requires a gradual process of restoration. But it's worthwhile to remember that in a family, the loving father is the one that disciplines.

In spite of the charges that we didn't love, we felt sure in our hearts that we did love. We came through this trial more committed to love and more convinced than ever that righteousness and mercy (or love) go hand in hand (see Psalm 85:10). It is incorrect to represent righteousness in opposition to love. Love is righteous, and love apart from righteousness is an absurdity, biblically impossible. We love righteousness and we want to love righteously.

Then we had to face another issue. I refer to the supposed conflict between the letter and the Spirit. As we tried to reason with our colleague about this problem we naturally used Scripture as a basis. Among our circle of pastors up to this time we never had heard the least insinuation that Scripture was relative. Scripture is absolute, our infallible guide. Of course, we did represent a movement of the Spirit. The Spirit of

God was very real to us; His presence, His voice, His authority was unquestioned. But we never pitted the authority of the Spirit against the authority of Scripture.

Now we were faced with charges that we were going back to the letter — the dead letter — of the Word. We heard declarations to the effect that "new" light had come. There were subtle insinuations that old words, though they had been adequate for other times, were mystically superceded by the active presence of the Spirit of God. This made us uneasy. We do believe that the letter by itself kills. But we do not have the letter alone; we have the Spirit. We love both the Word and the Spirit. We can err in interpreting both the Word and the voice of the Spirit, but as a foundational stance, we refuse to create a tension between the two. Frankly, if anything, we came through this trial more confirmed in the contemporary value of the written Word of God. We glory in the conviction that the Holy Spirit bears witness to our spirit that this is the truth.

FORGIVENESS AND RESTORATION

I want to enlarge upon one point that was engraved on our hearts as a consequence of our internal conflict. I mentioned the discrepancy over the question of considering that forgiveness was equivalent to restoration, especially with regards to a person who occupies a position of leadership in the church. We felt, of course, that forgiveness is surely proffered to any repentant person, but that forgiveness in itself does not qualify one for public ministry. As we mulled over this, we came up with at least six ingredients or factors that are necessary to qualify a person for pastoral ministry.

To begin with the individual must have an inner sense that God is leading him to assume such a responsibility. This involves inspiration or revelation, as well as personal commitment in submission and obedience to God. This is what some term "a call of God." Even in a minimum dose, the individual will have some conviction, some faith, that this is his vocation.

There should also be evidence of God's anointing, manifested in specific gifts for teaching, evangelism, etc. These are recognizable traits which indicate that the person is not simply "operating under his own steam."

Thirdly, there must be some knowledge — the more the better — of God's word and ways. This foundation in the unchanging truth gives assurance that the man's ministry and conduct will have Scriptural basis and content.

Fourthly, there must be maturity, good judgment, based upon personal experience as well as a sustained testimony of personal moral integrity. The Word of God specifies that an elder is not to be a novice. To govern the house of God, he must first govern his own family well. This is no small requisite, as it offers a sense of security and stability to those who will be presided over and ministered to by him.

This leads us to the next factor: there must be an approval and acceptance of his authority and leadership on the part of a group of people that is committed to him. This is simply to say that a person can hardly be a shepherd if he has no sheep. The saints cannot be obliged to accept the leadership of a man they do not know or cannot respect.

Finally, there should be a recognition or authorization on the part of those who exercise spiritual oversight for his life. Generally, this is first evidenced in the form of an ordination. It represents something of a guarantee of theological and moral integrity, in the terms by which this is understood among the ordaining body.

When one of these areas significantly breaks down, the man usually finds himself under question. And when this breakdown is in the area of immoral conduct, especially over a period of time, some of the other qualifications mentioned tend to break down as well. Loyalty and recognition of authority from the sheep usually give way. Generally, at this point, a group of pastors with recognized spiritual and ecclesiastical authority come on the scene to restore order, confidence, and authority. These are not simply arbitrary guidelines, but rather logical elements necessary to retain the integrity of the community. If they are not respected, then the community tends to become confused and may even disintegrate.

We could foresee the grave consequences of an insistence upon the doctrine that forgiveness is equivalent to complete restoration, especially when this was predicated upon an exaggerated position of unilateral priestly absolution and covering. The critical factor that validates priestly authority, enabling one to act and to speak in the name of the Almighty, is the fact of his continuing submission to the authority over him.

These convictions slowly but firmly developed in us as we passed through what seemed like a valley of shadows. We make no pretense of having totally satisfactory answers to all the questions raised. But we certainly have learned a lot, and the Lord has given abundant grace. The bond of unity between the pastors was sorely tried, but it stood the test. Although the problem with the brother mentioned had not yet been fully resolved — this came some time later — by mid-1975 the air was definitely clearer; relationships within the group of pastors as well as between the pastors and their leading men within the various congregations were much more precise; and our goals were more clearly defined. The fog had lifted and our focus was re-established.

GROUNDWORK FOR UNITY

"Therefore, strengthen the hands that are weak and the knees that are feeble, and make straight paths for your feet, so that the limb which is lame may not be put out of joint, but rather be healed."

— Hebrews 12:12, 13

Even before our small leaders' retreat in January, 1974, we had talked together frequently about the pros and cons of merging our various groups into one large congregation in the city of Buenos Aires. By and large, our sectarian and independent attitudes had been conquered through love, mutual confidence, and a significant work of the Holy Spirit in each of us. There remained, however, a lot of practical details to be settled, and we were still lacking a united, precise conviction as to what we should do about merger. The matter had not gotten much beyond the stage of serious conversation.

There were a number of things in favor of such a bold step. Obviously, it would be an effective answer to the oft-heard accusation that Christian congregations are not able to effectively work together on any long-term basis, or that pastors are usually hard-headed, self-sufficient individualists. It would be an approximation to the situation in the early church in Jerusalem, Antioch, etc., where the leadership was plural (twelve apostles in Jerusalem, prophets and teachers in Antioch, plural elders in other cities).

Hopefully, we could thus also avoid the one-sided "doctrinal-hobby" orientation of a group with a long-standing ministry from only one person. Our congregations would definitely profit from a better-balanced spiritual diet, and the pastors themselves would be able to receive as well as to give.

This, in turn, would make for a stronger, healthier community. It would clearly increase stability and aid toward maturity. Since solitude and heavy spiritual and psychological burdens are frequent sources of discouragement and downfall among pastors, a plural approach to pastoral responsibility and function offered an interesting alternative. Each one could also find greater freedom to concentrate on certain areas that needed more attention, such as giving time and training to leaders emerging in the community, or itinerant ministry, especially for the purpose of strengthening other groups in need, or opening new areas to the preaching of the Gospel. A broader and more effective counseling ministry could also be provided for the congregation.

Administratively, there were other advantages to be considered. By uniting in one large group, it would be unnecessary to pay for the upkeep of several different physical plants. In any case, we were already de-emphasizing the need for many large meetings in favor of a multiplicity of smaller home meetings. We had come to realize that one large meeting a week was sufficient if the saints were properly related in smaller neighborhood communities through the week. These groups should be small enough to know everyone by first name, care for each other and keep in touch regarding a multitude of varied interests. This direction in our activities was already strengthening the families in the congregation.

We could see that on the horizon of our experience of the church as the Body of Christ in Argentina, some radical developments were coming in relation to the saints meeting from house to house, and living normal lives as a community, as a people, being a light in the darkness of their neighborhood. All this would tend to develop leaders without the ecclesiastical trimmings so common in both evangelical and catholic circles. We were yearning to give more attention to this area, yet we were finding ourselves almost prisoners of the church systems we had inherited. There was precious little opportunity to be spontaneous, to be real and sincere, to be normal, to spend time with family and with friends in order to get acquainted, to work and play together. With a steady round of church functions, there is little spare time for simply living and enjoying life.

One thing was clear to us as we appraised these possibilities and longings: it would not be enough simply to merge our various congregations. This alone could conceivably depersonalize the people as they were lost in the crowd. No, in order for the merger to be a step forward it would necessarily have to be accompanied with a reorientation of the people in relatively small face-to-face communities. One can easily get lost in the shuffle of a thousand or more people, but he can hardly get lost in a small home!

HARD QUESTIONS

While there were clearly advantages, we were not naively plunging ahead toward a utopian dream. There were some hard questions to be answered. How would a group of pastors function together, when for years each one had been "King Bee" in his own empire? What about a typical pastor's tendency to view his pulpit ministry as nearly all-important? How would he justify to his well-trained sense of self-esteem the prospect of just "warming a bench" for two or three Sundays in a row?

How would salaries be determined? Who would have the final word in a dispute? If we got all the sheep together into one pen, which sheep would belong to which shepherd? What part would loyalty play, if any?

Who would hire and who would fire pastors and other back-up ministries? Since some men rather obviously "outshine" others, who is to say that some of the less brilliant or less aggressive ones would not be significantly overshadowed? Would the new structure not tend to become rather monolithic or legalistic as the stronger ones imposed their viewpoints upon the larger community? And if this were so, would we not likely face the tragedy of new splits and disgruntled factions?

And what about the great distances that separated our various congregations? Some of the saints were more than two hours' distance from each other. Buenos Aires is an immense metropolitan area with about eleven million people! Public transportation is normally quite reliable and abundant, but to mobilize a family of four or five when they have to take a bus, then a train and another bus just to get to a three-hour meeting, takes a sizeable bite out of the family budget and requires a strong and continued motivation to keep it up week after week. And most of the families in Argentina do not have either a car or a telephone.

GAINING EXPERIENCE AND CONFIDENCE

Some time earlier we had gotten to the stage in our conversations of taking some tentative steps in this direction. For one thing, we had gained enough experience and confidence in working together that we really did trust each other. One or two on the periphery had some doubts, but we were not inclined to pressure anyone toward such a step. Give them time — we reasoned — and love and confidence will replace fears and reserves.

At one point we decided to spend a few days together in the western suburb of Moreno to pray and talk over our first moves toward merger. Most of us had already primed the principal families — our mainstay of support — in our own congregations. We had the confidence that they would go with us all the way. Still it seemed like a terribly big bite to take all at once. So we concluded that our first step toward merger should involve only four groups that were meeting in the capitol city of Buenos Aires proper.

The rest of us were in the suburban areas. For the moment our participation would be mainly in terms of ministry and counsel in this first merger. The idea was that as they worked their way through the initial adjustments we would all learn. We were thinking in terms of then adding the suburban groups to the larger group in the capitol whenever the time seemed right.

TO MERGE OR NOT TO MERGE

In January of 1974, however, the climate for advance along this line did not look favorable. The difficulty mentioned in the former chapter was beginning to cloud the picture. Several felt discouraged and rather disconcerted about the feasibility of moving ahead. With these factors arrayed against any merger of the congregations, the issue tended to fade.

Except in Ivan and Jorge. Disturbed over our loss of enthusiasm and faith for the project, they began to pray together and talk over the possibility of bringing their two groups together. Ivan's people, having begun inauspiciously in their home, had now considerably increased in number, with several dynamic and growing home meetings. They were constantly winning others. The pragmatic approach of their pastor, his diligence in getting all the saints out witnessing, his insistence upon active lay leadership, and his clear sense of objectives, were proving quite successful.

Unlike Jorge, Ivan's approach was not

markedly charismatic. Their meetings, for instance, were not especially strong in worship. After getting "burned" with some extremes among a few of his own people, Ivan had decided to back off a bit from the more mystical angle. Through his own example, he had impressed upon his people the preeminence of personal work, in teaching as well as in evangelism. They had no special need or use for pulpits or special buildings or for an order of service. They were activists, with no great enthusiasm for big meetings.

While Jorge was certainly in favor of this kind of home-based, face-to-face activity, he was a 'bell-ringer' in the pulpit. By this I do not mean spectacular or showy, but eloquent, clear-thinking, very adept in communicating his thoughts in such a way as to inspire action. Also, over the years Jorge and I had spent much time together and our spirits were closely knit. I had constantly communicated to him my own deep conviction as to the central place of worship among God's people, and I had shared with him my own twenty-odd years of experience in moving under the anointing of the Holy Spirit.

Jorge had become "prophetic" in his own rights, in the sense of having a clear word from the Lord, of calling the people of God to a real confrontation with the Almighty, of denouncing sin and promoting holiness and a sincere love for the Lord. Jorge had strong and well-trained gifts for active leadership, and he was not one to stand along the side-lines and look in.

When the rest of us learned that Ivan and Jorge were in the talking stage of a merger between the two, I think many of us rather expected the sparks to fly. Both were strong-minded men. Both had loyal congregations. Either one would be a leader in whatever enterprise he tackled. Without the easier manner of a Keith Bentson as a liaison, for instance, they could run into problems. Evidently, this union would be a tough test for our theories and convictions about spiritual unity.

Jorge's father, a godly and faithful man of deep fervor and dedication, laid down a condition to his son when it was clear they would bring together the two groups. "One thing, Jorge, I beg of you," he declared, "Don't 'water-down' the worship!"

APRIL IN FLORES

At last, in April, the dramatic step was taken. The two congregations started meeting on Sundays, with the leadership of two pastors instead of one. It was not, however, a total union; not for several months, until all the folk felt sure of the move. The various home groups continued to function separately. When new converts were added, the baptisms and subsequent integration was effected basically at the level of the home groups. The administration of funds was kept separate between the two larger congregations, as well as the support of the two pastors and their financial commitments toward missions, the poor, etc.

This separation of responsibilities was not because of doubts about whether the union would last; rather, it was a caution against trying to tackle too many problems at once. "Let's take a step at a time" — they reasoned — but every step became a stronger confirmation of the rightness of it all. Within a year, the merger had become a new way of life for the participants. They no longer referred to themselves according to their original groupings. Increasingly, they were becoming known as the congregation of Flores (the name of the political subdivision or "barrio" as it is called in Spanish). In reality, their people were coming from many parts of suburban Buenos Aires, as well as from the capitol city. And before long, Ivan's original group from Casanova had joined them also.

Perhaps most interesting of all is the fact that, to this day, Ivan and Jorge are delighted to be together. Both say they have yet to have their first real dispute. Problems they have had: disciplinary measures, burdens, needs of the poor, the need for strategic decisions; but no discord has come between these two men of God.

For one thing, from the outset, Jorge — being the younger by over fifteen years — set himself to respect Ivan as the older and more mature of the two. Ivan has a beautiful family and home life, exemplary in so many ways. Jorge and his wife Silvia realized that with their young preschoolers they could learn much from Ivan and Gloria with their teen-agers.

Jorge has the custom of expressing his convictions with faith, but will not force an issue. He sees Ivan in the place of spiritual responsibility over him, his personal pastor. Far from squelching Jorge, this relationship has definitely enhanced his ministry.

Ivan is an excellent trouble-shooter, pinpointing problems in different home groups and in struggling believers. As Jorge laid before him the various situations in which he had encountered problems or where growth had been stunted, Ivan helped him to make proper diagnosis and correction. One by one, adjustments were made in Jorge's various home groups until they began to be more effective and fruitful, winning new converts and nurturing them toward maturity.

As Ivan's input tended to turn the whole group outward in dynamic and constant extension and witness, Jorge's input seemed to be more in terms of turning them upward to God in worship and consecration, through a strong teaching ministry. I should not labor this point, since both tendencies have long been evident in them both. Yet it is true that Jorge's folk became more effective in their witness to others, even as Ivan's people became more dynamic in worship and in walking in the Spirit, clearly results of the merger.

This delightful combination of the practical with the spiritual, of the evangelistic element with the charismatic opened up further vistas in regards to the ministry of the Word. Jorge began to share some of the new insights in the weekly pastors' meetings. They were so evidently "just what we needed" that the feeling among the pastors was unanimous that we needed to call a three-day retreat in order for Jorge and Ivan to open up this whole new area to us. This we did in August, 1974.

14

BUILDING WITH THE WORD

"Built upon the foundation of the apostles and prophets, Christ Jesus Himself being the corner stone."

— Ephesians 2:20

The retreat we had in the town of José C. Paz in August, 1974 merits a chapter to itself. It was a true watershed. In retrospect, it seems to us now that until then we were getting the pieces of a puzzle together, yet without really understanding their relationship to each other. Now the various parts of the picture were coming together and we were beginning to see their inter-relationship within the larger context.

To put it another way, we saw clearly the need to build, not just work or keep active. We needed to build lives, to build families, to build the church. New people were turning to the Lord that needed to be incorporated into the family of the faithful. Meetings were not enough; sermons were not enough. Fellowship was not enough. We could not simply depend upon a passing inspiration to get the job done. Christians can be on a mountain-top in a glorious gathering, but they soon descend into the valley of everyday existence and struggles. Down there, how do they live?

Paul was a wise master-builder — an architect — that laid the foundation and directed the subsequent building process. He warned others that if they built carelessly, there would be loss. Materials for the construction of a home cannot be just thrown into place without coordination. The work cannot be directed by incompetent people. The entire building project must follow a predetermined plan and be carried out by able workers. We, too, wanted to build wisely.

A FIRM FOUNDATION

It was a chilly winter day when we gathered on the beautiful grounds of the Catholic retreat center recently completed in the northern suburb of José C. Paz. The center is maintained by the "Focolares," a renewal movement within the Roman Catholic Church. They had welcomed us for previous gatherings and made us feel so comfortable that we were happy to return. The main building is far enough away from the hustle and bustle of the highway and passing cars, set in the midst of lovely lawns and tall Eucaliptus trees, so that we found the setting ideal for contemplation, for prayer, for "tuning in" to the voice of God.

Jorge had shared enough with us in a couple previous Monday night meetings to whet our appetites for more. We all had the sense that things were getting into focus, and we opened our hearts and our ears to listen to the Lord's messenger.

The first thing to be considered was the FOUNDATION of spiritual life and of the church. This foundation is Jesus Christ, God's revelation, God's word, to all men. Jorge pointed to Hebrews, chap. 1: "In these last days God has spoken to us in His Son." He said that the main instrument that Christ used to reveal His Father's will and truth was the spoken word. And the only record we have of His words is that which His apostles communicated, either directly or through other writers (Mark and Luke).

"Jesus left no message or record behind except what His word and His life engraved on the minds and hearts of His chosen followers," Jorge reminded us. "He was obviously not very concerned that they make great efforts to remember everything. He assured them that the

Holy Spirit would bring to their minds the things He had told them. This fact — said Jorge — must be underlined: Jesus trusted implicitly in the Holy Spirit to remind, to teach, to reveal and to guide them in all truth. Apart from this confidence in the Spirit of God, His failure to register things more carefully would appear to be irresponsible.

"Yet it was this very confidence that placed the greater burden upon His apostles. It was they who, after His resurrection and the outpouring of the Holy Spirit, were to carry His life and His truth everywhere, making disciples of all nations, preaching, baptizing and teaching all who responded to do everything that Jesus commanded them. That is to say, the instructions and the commands that Christ gave to His apostles were the very instructions and commands that they were to pass on to all others who followed in His train. They need not worry about elaborating a body of truth; they had to simply give to others what Christ had given to them. The same Holy Spirit that had made this truth live in them would also work in others for the same purpose."

The focus that this gave to Christian discipleship was not lost on us. We began to see that our main responsibility was to know and understand what Christ taught His twelve apostles and then to see what they taught to other disciples. This, then, is essentially what we were to teach. These truths are fundamental, foundational, and the foundation has not changed. Nor will it change in the future! Paul made it very clear that there is only one foundation, and to tamper with that foundation is to invite an anathema!

Neither is that foundation to be modified, corrected or adjusted in any way. Yet it goes without saying that it can be clarified, its significance amplified, its truth applied to new and varying situations. The later epistles in the Scriptures seem more concerned about underlining the everlasting truths already set forth, or about calling people to repentance for having left the foundation once laid, than in presenting new truths.

Still, the history of Christianity over nearly twenty centuries presents the lamentable picture of grave departures from the faith set forth by Christ and His apostles, of distortion, of ignorance and of apostasy. It is this fact that gives credibility and validity to every genuine movement toward spiritual renewal, awakening and restoration. The Holy Spirit is calling His people to recover that which Christ and His apostles set forth with clarity, conviction and power.

Jorge reminded us that we are witnesses to the fact that God is presently accelerating this movement toward the total restoration of the church. He insisted that this is evidenced in three ways: (1) Rather than restoring isolated truths, the Holy Spirit is recovering the entire scope of God's truth and purpose. (2) No longer are we seeing only local and isolated revivals or awakenings; an extensive, globe-covering spiritual renewal is taking place in our day. (3) It is also clear that we are not dealing simply with a recovery of certain concepts or theories; obviously, the Lord is moving to raise up a people for himself, a community that lives according to the teaching of Christ. That is to say, more important than simply announcing or believing a truth, the Lord is pointing up the need for us to experience and live out the truth received.

He concluded his discourse on the foundation, pointing out that today the vision is clearer, purer and more dynamic than ever before. To that we all heartily agreed! Then he urged us to give ourselves without reserve to the Lord so that He might fully realize His purpose in us.

A POWERFUL HEAVENLY FORCE

Having primed the pump, we were anxious for the next session to begin! Jorge commenced by stating, "There are two concrete elements that God has given for the edification of the church. Put quite simply, they are the apostolic preaching and the apostolic doctrine. Both are the word of God, but their function is different."

In both Spanish and English the meaning of the Greek words translated preaching and doctrine is not immediately apparent. Therefore, Jorge gave us the original words in Greek and for most of the remainder of the retreat these words were used with increasing familiarity: kerygma and didache.

Defining these words, he told us that kerygma is the anointed and authoritative proclamation of the person and work of Christ, present and active among men, for the purpose of leading them to faith for their salvation and transformation. This kerygma — or proclamation — is an erruption of the spirit, a powerful heavenly force; therefore, it can hardly be adequately expressed in the calculated atmosphere of an academic classroom. Rather, it is manifested in the warmth of the believing church, whether in the great assembly of the saints or among the two or three gathered in Christ's name, or in the preaching of the good news to sinful men. "The herald who makes this proclamation" — said Jorge — "is not to be a mechanical repeater of the rudiments of the Christian message, but a man afire with the Spirit."

And he continued: "This kerygma has a dynamic function. It is a supernatural phenomenon. When a person believes the proclamation and confesses it, the truth becomes operative in him. He has not simply received an idea or a fact; he has received a truth that is alive, a truth that operates powerfully within him, quickening and inflaming his inner being by the Holy Spirit, for the Spirit and the kerygma are inseparable. This is the reason Paul can speak of the power of 'hearing with faith' (Rom. 10:8-10, 17 and Gal. 3:2, 5). The kerygma provokes and inspires faith, life, grace: an experience with God here and now!

"This kerygma is a proclamation of what is already a reality, an eternal verity. It is clear, definitive, complete. It is neither vague, nor indefinable, nor interminable. We can only believe it or reject it; we cannot argue with it. It is not presented for our consideration; it is proclaimed for our salvation. The heart of this proclamation is the death and resurrection of Christ. To some this is a stumbling block and to others it is foolishness; but to those who believe, it is the power of God and the wisdom of God (I Cor. 1:18-25). This kerygma, then, imposes upon us a three-fold responsibility: we must know it; we must believe it; and we must proclaim it."

THE WILL OF GOD FOR OUR LIVES

Next, Jorge clarified the biblical meaning of doctrine, didache, stating that the concepts he was now going to share with us he had learned essentially from Ivan, in the teaching he gave to the new disciples. Here again, our traditional ideas ill-equipped us to understand the real meaning of the word. Underlining the words of Jesus in Matthew 7:24-29 and of Paul in Titus 2:1-15, Jorge said: "The didache consists of teaching, instructions, and the clear commands of Christ, whose essential characteristic is that they reveal the will of God for our lives. The didache — or apostolic doctrine — is imperative: we not only hear . . . we must do, we must obey. The didache is not complicated; it is not difficult to understand. It is simple and it is clear.

"Neither is it a never-ending string of concepts. Scripture never gives us the impression that the didache is interminable. It is a concrete body of instructions; it is communicable, it is understandable, it can be applied and obeyed. Jesus instructed His apostles that they were to teach others to 'observe all that I commanded you' (Matt. 28:20). Paul could later say to the brothers from Ephesus that he had declared to them 'the whole purpose of God' (Acts 20:26, 27). And he reminded Timothy that he was to communicate to others what Paul had communicated to him (II Tim. 2:2). Clearly, obedience is expected on the basis of clearly-presented instructions."

Jorge continued: "Paul, Peter, and John all indicate that the same instructions are to be repeated again and again; they do not become useless or outdated with age or repetition (Phil. 3:1; II Pet. 1:12-15; I Jn. 2:7, 8). The same words are used many times and are useful for exhortation, for admonition and for reproof" (see Rom. 15:14; Col. 3:16; Phil. 4:9; etc.).

Jorge then showed us the process whereby the didache becomes operative in us: "First of all, we must know it, hear it, grasp its significance with our minds and understand it. Secondly, we obey, we do, we apply it specifically to given areas of our lives. This requires faith, diligence, self-discipline. This in turn gives room to the Holy Spirit to incarnate the will of God in our lives and thus fashion us increasingly in the image of Jesus Christ. Finally, having taken it to heart so that it has become a part of us, it is then our responsibility to communicate it to others."

This session was concluded as Jorge pointed out our need for three essential elements: (1) Clear vision. We must have precise concepts. Unclear commands, fuzzy ideas render obedience impossible and frustrate rather than enlighten. (2) Profound conviction. This is only possible when one can say that he is sure that something is of God. We must be able to say, "God said this." (3) Unwavering determination. We must take God at His word and obey, regardless of the consequences. Human reasoning or sentiment must not be allowed to neutralize the commands of Christ.

Then he gave us a simple and unforgettable definition of a Christian disciple: "It is someone who BELIEVES all that Christ said and DOES all that Christ commands. We must believe the proclamation of the Gospel and obey the doctrine of Christ."

FAITH IS THE KEY

Next Jorge illustrated for us the relationship between the kerygma and the didache, between truth and the commandments. These two elements constitute the essence of the word of God.

"Why is it that Christians so frequently find God's commandments heavy and unpalatable? — Jorge queried. — "Why do we find it so easy to make excuses and cover-ups for not implicitly obeying God's revealed will? Many are unable to say with the apostle John, 'His commandments are not burdensome' (I Jn. 5:3).

"When this is the case, the missing element is faith. Faith is the key that relates the kerygma and the didache. Let's see how this works in practice.

"First, the truth — eternal and unchanging — is proclaimed. The open heart responds in faith. The truth generates faith, which then becomes operative in the life. On the basis of this truth the Holy Spirit ministers grace to those who believe. This grace brings life, power, hope, a supernatural element which makes possible changes, adjustments and the discipline which God requires of us. The proclamation of the truth clears away the confusion, fears, and doubts, and one begins to see things differently. The heart and the will become favorably disposed toward the will of God.

"This grace is not simply for our enjoyment;

its purpose is to effect the will of God in our lives, conforming us to Christ's image. Paul declares to Titus that grace instructs us to 'deny ungodliness and worldly desires and to live sensibly, righteously and godly in the present age . . .' (Titus 2:11-15). This grace is not to be received in vain, that is, without purpose or effect.

"When grace and faith become operative in us through the proclamation and reception of the truth, then we must have the commandments and instructions that make the truth relevant in specific areas and situations of our lives. The abstract becomes specific; that which is general becomes particular; grace and faith are applied to defined areas. In this way the Spirit of God effects in us the mind of Christ and we are conformed to His image. Christ living in me works in me to bring all things under His gracious rule. As this happens, I find fulfillment, real joy, a sense of realization. My humanity becomes the channel whereby Christ is able to reveal Himself through me to the world around. This is a gradual process that takes place throughout the course of our lives."

Jorge underlined the fact that the exercise of our wills, in the alignment of our lives with the will of God, is essential: "We cannot take a passive attitude. When faith is present, my will chooses to obey. We believe, and therefore we obey. Where obedience is lacking, faith is generally inoperative or wavering.

"For instance, John declares that we love God because He first loved us (I Jn. 4:19). We are commanded to love God with all our hearts, minds and strength. But there is no motivation within us to obey the command until we learn that God first loved us. When that truth is declared and received in faith, we find it easy and enjoyable to give ourselves wholly to God in love. The commandment is no longer burdensome.

"Likewise, if we are told that the will of God is

that we give thanks in all things, the command seems totally unreasonable unless we know and believe that God is all-wise and benevolent, making everything work together for good to those that are called according to His purpose. Moreover, when this truth is further illustrated with case histories from the Bible or from our contemporaries, faith responds and channels obedience, so that it no longer seems foolish to rejoice in every circumstance. It is our simple and loving response to our Father's good will."

In quick review, Jorge reminded us that "we must proclaim the truth with faith so that it penetrates. But if edification is to take place, there must be adjustment, instruction in righteousness, discipline, because our lives in their natural state are not aligned with God's will. In Romans chapter 6, Paul outlines the tight relationship that exists between grace and obedience, and in our daily lives this relationship must be operative. Faith is the key. This faith produces good works that glorify our Father in heaven."

The entire retreat was a profound lesson in practical theology. The sessions just concluded already had our hearts pounding in anticipation, and all of us were making a hasty mental review of our preaching and teaching, aware of the need for adjustments and corrections. The whole presentation was so plausible that there was really no questioning of the basic tenets. On the contrary, our understanding of the Gospel of the kingdom and of the need to build the saints together in a functioning corporate relationship had set the stage for the application of these truths. But the retreat was not over yet.

A DOOR, A GOAL, AND A WAY

"Jesus said to him, "I am the way, and the truth, and the life; no one comes to the Father, but through Me."

— John 14:6

In the remaining sessions Jorge and Ivan shared together the ministry. Comparing John 14:6 with various passages in the book of Acts (9:2, 19:9, 23; 22:4; 24:14, 22) they pointed out that, "the early Christians spoke of their walk and relationship with the Lord and with each other as the WAY. The idea given is that of a pathway, a walk, a life-style, a pattern of behavior. Essentially, the figure is that of a road or highway leading to a destination. Obviously, every pathway has a starting point and a terminal point." With this, we began to focus on the three essential elements that the early believers discerned in their understanding and practical application of the kingdom of God in their lives: a DOOR, a WAY, and a GOAL.

The entrance — or door — would involve all that was necessary to believe or to do in order to get started on the journey toward the goal. From the experience of the church on the day of its birth at Pentecost, as well as in subsequent situations, we saw that this entrance included the clear proclamation of the Gospel concerning the person and work of Christ, the response of convicted hearts in faith, their obedience in repentance and baptism, and their reception of the Holy Spirit. This composite experience got them into a right relationship with God and set them on their way. In a word, to begin meant a total commitment to Jesus Christ as Lord.

TO BE LIKE JESUS

Before we could concentrate on the way itself, we realized that we had to define the objective, the goal of the Christian life. We already realized that heaven was not the goal, but part of the reward. The objective, we understood, had to be in line with God's original intention for man in the act of creation. God's eternal purpose could not have changed as a result of man's disobedience or fall. Redemption through the blood of Christ is the heart of God's plan of recovery for fallen man; but this is the means, not the goal.

The goal was declared by God Himself in his creative decree, and then reiterated time and again in the Scriptures (Gen. 1:26, 27; Rom. 8:28, 29; I Cor. 11:7; II Cor. 3:18; Col. 3:10). The objective is conformity to God's image. The Bible makes it clear that this image relationship in man involves moral responsibility, a spiritual nature, and the exercise of dominion or authority over creation. God has purposed that we be like Him, at least in these areas. And the Holy Spirit is at work in our lives to bring us into the good of all this.

In this manner, the character and the works of Christ are to be manifested in human lives, right here on the face of the earth. The goal is not only for the "sweet by-and-by"; it's for the "nasty now-and-now". God has purposed to reveal Christ to the world through a redeemed people, through men and women who live in His will, who shine with His grace, who rejoice in His love. And this revelation is not given through preaching alone, but through the life-style, the behavior, the good deeds of those who are being conformed to the image of Christ. The Father wants a large family of children who are like Jesus. For this purpose He has adopted us as His dear children, and is working constantly in our lives, through His truth and His commandments, through the Holy Spirit, through the fellowship of the saints.

So many things were now coming into focus that we wondered if we didn't need more time just to assimilate all these facets. Our minds were dashing along a heavenly race-track, but we were aware that we had yet to get it all together here on earthly sod. Still there was more to come.

REORIENTING THE LIFE-STYLE

It was time to consider the pathway between the entrance and the objective. Having started out in the Christian life we set our sights on the goal of being like Christ. But how do we get there? Here we began to see the practical significance of Christ's doctrine, or didache. Jesus had fully revealed the Father's will and purpose to the apostles, through His own life-style and teaching. After His ascension and the glorious descent of the Holy Spirit, they were empowered to teach in the same way as Christ had. Following His own mandate they began to teach the new believers — or disciples — "all that He had commanded them." Their instructions were clear and unequivocal. They taught with authority. Anointed by the heavenly Spirit they proclaimed eternal verities with deep conviction. When the sword of the Spirit struck the hearts of their hearers, causing them to cry out for forgiveness and release from their burden, they were told to "repent and be baptized." Immediately the new believers received the gift of the Holy Spirit and begun to long for a total reorientation in their life-style.

Having been told that they needed to be "saved from this perverse generation," the Bible tells us that, following their baptism, "they were continually devoting themselves to the apostles' teaching (didache) and to fellowship . . . " (Acts 2:42). Their wholehearted obedience was evidenced in their selfless surrender of earthly possessions and their sincere commitment to each other. Christ was thus living out His life through them as they walked in obedience and in the Holy Spirit.

As the years passed, the early apostles had occasion to put into writing many of the instructions they gave to the disciples, both to individual believers and to whole assemblies in different parts of the world. These letters — or epistles — were treasured by the early Christians to the point that during the decades of intense persecution by the Roman emperors many of them gave their lives simply for the crime of possessing copies of these apostolic writings.

In the teaching of the apostles we find many of Christ's own earlier teachings elucidated and applied. Having been taught by Christ Himself, their own teaching acquired a value that is still appreciated more than nineteen centuries later. The social context has often changed; the intellectual condition of the readers or hearers has greatly varied; but the teaching of Christ and His apostles is timeless and just as valid today for each of us as it was for Galilean fishermen, Jewish tax-collectors, or Roman centurions.

APOSTOLIC TEACHING

As Ivan and Jorge brought us face to face with these facts, their significance loomed large in our immediate context. Our initial task was now to review all the recorded instructions that Christ gave to His disciples, or to the multitudes that followed Him, as well as all the teachings registered in the ministry of the apostles.

We decided to be intensely practical about all this. So in one of the sessions at the retreat we separated into three or four different groups, our purpose being to make a quick overview of all these teachings, grouping them according to subjects treated. In conclusion, each of the groups was to present in the following session a rough classification under different headings of all the instructions given by Christ or the apostles. Of course, because of the limited time we had, no pretense was made to be thorough or profound. The idea was simply to introduce us to the subject matter.

When we all got together again, we discovered that there were only minor variations between the conclusions of the different groups. We saw that the biblical injunctions could be divided under such headings as instructions on prayer, family, civil responsibility, money, morality, fraternal relationships, etc. We concluded that though the list was lengthy, it was not interminable. Certainly it was not hazy or uncertain.

Jorge then suggested that we had a serious responsibility to dedicate a considerable part of our time together in the coming months to review in detail these very teachings, until in our minds the apostolic teaching was crystal-clear. In the process we needed to give ourselves to instructing and repeating these same commands and teaching intensively, until there was evidence that all were taking seriously this word from the Lord. Only so could we be really sure that we were being built together according to the will of God.

The whole thought and purpose was alive with hope and possibilities. We could see that it was analogous to building a house. When the plans are known and followed, you know where to start, how to proceed and when the work is done. The building of the house or the people of God was certainly more complex, but it need not be confusing or uncertain.

THE LESSONS GROW

Consequently, following the retreat several of

Pastors from Buenos Aires en route to Chile in 1972.

Pastors' Retreat in Cordob province in 1975.

Mealtime at Embalse, Dick is in the center with a beard, 1977.

Retreat at Embalse in 1978. Bruce Longstregth is to the left, Charles Simpson is in the center, Author is on the right.

Bob Mumford preaching at the Retreat in Embalse in 1978. Ivan Baker, to the right, is interpreting.

Charles Simpson preaching at Embalse in 1978. Hugo Zelaya is interpreting.

Keith Bentson, 1979.

Pastor Angel Negro, 1979.

Jorge Himitian in Freeville, NY, 1979.

us decided to start meeting together one morning each week to get into this study. We first outlined the project before us, determining broadly what we had to do. We decided to stipulate a week in advance the subject matter to be reviewed each Wednesday morning, so that we all had time for personal preparation and study. After discussion and general agreement, the material would be collected in outline form for preparation of printed lessons. Each one would be accompanied with memory verses from the Scriptures, so as to engrave on the mind of each disciple the word of the Lord.

Jorge prepared a written introduction and the first set of lessons on the DOOR of salvation. He and I worked together on the lesson on God's eternal purpose, the GOAL. Then together with a number of pastors we decided to prepare the first set of lessons on the WAY, or the Christian walk, around the general heading of the "old life and the new." Guided by our experience in working with the newly converted, we endeavored to set down the main areas of sin and darkness they must overcome and what the Scriptures have to say about these areas, how to be free and how to walk in obedience to the Lord. In successive lessons, we dealt with such things as sexual uncleanness, pride, dishonesty, pessimism, the occult, injustices, etc.; all of them being areas which are prominent problems in our Latin society.

The second series of lessons we prepared under the general heading of "Relationships between Christians," involving seven lessons. The third series was on the family. There is still much to be done, but we have found the study enlightening and enriching to all of us and quite useful in teaching others. From time to time we revise or polish up the lessons, but retain the simple outline form. Our idea has been basically to provide practical printed material for use in the nearly 100 home meetings around the city.

The home leaders are first taught the material by their pastors and then they in turn use it as they sense the need for it. These lessons form the basis for discussion and application; they are not designed for the preparation of sermons.

Some wondered if this approach in teaching and edification wouldn't result in a stereotyped, mechanical system. Perhaps that would happen if the groups should become ingrown. But with normal and steady growth, the influx of new converts serves to keep things alive and interesting. By the time any given set of lessons has been presented, discussed and applied, there is a new group of hungry disciples just converted who are anxious to learn and to grow in their new-found Christian life. A kind of chain-reaction takes place as those recently taught share with those recently converted.

All this work in the preparation of lesson material and the training of the home leaders kept us pretty well occupied for months. It was about this time (1974 and 1975) that many Christian circles — and especially the charismatic movement in general — were being shaken up over the rapidly spreading concepts of discipleship, authority and submission, etc. So we decided it was just as well that we "keep our heads down" and do our homework. This may well have been what saved us from falling into the serious conflicts that marred relationships among Christians in many parts of the world.

16

DIFFICULTIES AND DEFINITIONS

"And He said to them, "Come away by yourselves to a lonely place and rest awhile."

— Mark 6:31

Without any effort to correlate what was happening among us in Argentina with what was happening elsewhere, by 1973 our paths were crossing in a mutually beneficial interchange with leaders in the U.S.A., England, and several South American countries. As mentioned in an earlier chapter, several of us had traveled and ministered beyond our borders concerning the things set forth in this book. In almost every place we had been very well received. We found our hearts being closely knit with many servants of the Lord whom we highly respected. It was evident to us that "this thing was not done in a corner." What the Lord was working out in us, He was also doing elsewhere.

We have learned much from our brethren in other lands, and feel that our input has been likewise appreciated. The months of October and November, 1973 were especially significant, in that Juan Carlos, Keith, and I were all ministering at the same time — albeit in different places — in the U.S.A. We were aware, also, that various pastors there were moving in similar ways to ourselves. It seemed clear to us all that the Spirit of God was awakening his people around the world with truths that were intended to revitalize our witness and our labor, as well as to break down sectarian barriers between us.

But things were not to continue peacefully for long. Stories got started, some church leaders got up in arms, distortions and exaggerations abounded, and things looked furious for a season.

In the U.S., by 1975 it was an "open secret" that the charismatics were badly divided over such issues as spiritual authority and submission and certain concepts of discipleship. Although we had never been completely without hostile glances from certain church groups in Argentina, we were not facing the open conflicts and attacks that were raging in the United States.

As we viewed the difficult situation there from a distance, we also realized that with all that Jorge had "laid on us" during the retreat in José C. Paz, we had plenty to do locally. It seemed wise that we consciously lower our profile — talk and write less, travel less — and give ourselves to doing our homework. As it turned out, it was a godsend. 1975 was a very significant year for us. Looking back upon the course of events from that time onward, I think it is a proper evaluation to say that our roots were already down by then and rather firm, but the Lord purposed to firm up our relationships at the pastoral level, get us all involved in making disciples in the homes and invigorate our evangelistic outreach. For that is what happened in the following months.

CLARIFYING VERTICAL RELATIONSHIPS

Bob Mumford visited us for six days in May of 1975. Although his prime concern was to help us to resolve some problems (referred to in chap. 12), he agreed to minister during a brief retreat with about a hundred ministers, including some of their wives.

Bob began by saying that much of what he intended to share with us during those days were things that he had heard already from some of us whom he had met in the U.S. But when they came out of his mouth and his spirit, they came with his own inimitable vigorous style. Everything he said was received as "fresh bread." It was no warmed-over meal. Obviously, the Lord had been deeply working in him, just as in us, for the sense of union and fellowship at a deep level was experienced by all.

He opened up a new area for us also, exhorting us to give more attention to our vertical relationships with each other. Up to that time, we had often said that all the pastors in the group functioned with the same level of authority. This was not entirely realistic; rather, it was the expression of an ideal. In actual practice, just by the nature of things, there were different measures of grace and ministry. Still, we made a point of testifying that together we formed a plural pastorate, all on the same level. While there were advantages in that no one 'lorded it over' another, on occasion we found it a bit impractical. It was easy to 'pass the buck', as no one was clearly in charge and no one was specifically responsible for coordinating things. Consequently, things often got unnecessarily delayed in the execution.

Bob insisted that this issue should be clarified among us, as it would help us to move ahead and get on with the task the Lord had given us. It would also make it easier for each one to find his proper place in relation to the rest. Whatever gift or ministry a person had would be enhanced if he had a proper and workable relationship with others in the Body of Christ.

About a month later, nearly twenty of us pastors went into "conclave" for three days to pray and talk over this matter. Our purpose was basically to find out how each one felt about the issue and about his relationship with the rest of the pastors. We needed to know, too, how many felt a clear commitment to the rest in terms of the ways the Lord had been leading us. Was there a consensus regarding the issue of vertical authority among us? Should we spell things out more clearly in this respect?

A few days prior to this retreat six of us had

spent a day together in prayer and fasting. Of the group of pastors we were the only ones of the original group dating back to 1967 when we started meeting together. The idea of our meeting was suggested by the rest in order for us to draw up some guide-lines for better understanding of our relationships. The fact that we were the older veterans of the group would hopefuly give a wider perspective to the situation facing us at the moment. The main thing we concluded was that no matter what course things took, we intended to stand together.

As we met together on the first day of the conclave, the first item on the agenda was to spend the entire initial session in prayer. We earnestly sought the Lord to enlighten our minds and hearts and to lead us in a plain path.

In the following session each man voiced the nature of his commitment to the rest. Two of the pastors who had long stood with us would soon be leaving the country to live elsewhere, and a third had some reservations about committing himself beyond a simple fraternal relationship. The remainder, however, seemed firm in their resolve to move ahead together. As a matter of fact, one after another stated that, essentially, nothing was changing since he already had a clear and firm commitment toward the rest of the group.

THE "SOFT KNIFE"

Then we discussed the question of the need for some specific vertical authority within the group. The general feeling was not that we needed to designate a new authority, but that we should recognize those who had spiritual ascendancy among us. All the brothers were asked to seriously consider the whole matter. In the next gathering we would all write down on individual slips of paper the names of the pastors that each one recognized as having spiritual authority within the group.

Underlying this decision was the conviction that we should not go beyond what was an existing reality; nothing should be forced or improvised. What we aimed to do was simply declare openly as a group what was latent until then. In order for such a decision to be valid, it would need to be something that sprang spontaneously out of the heart of each man.

The consensus among the pastors was unanimous. It was quite obvious that some, by simple gravitation of their ministry and maturity, were clearly recognized by all as having spiritual ascendancy among the pastors. Moreover, all of us agreed that Keith Bentson was the man that God had placed among us to preside and coordinate.

After that, something that had gradually developed among us in a natural and spontaneous way surfaced in the group consciousness: in reality, there were different levels of ministry and authority among us. In this, we felt there was a similarity to the situation in Antioch: "Now there were at Antioch . . . prophets and teachers . . . " (Acts 13:1). From then on, Keith would function as our coordinator. He would be responsible to see that what needed to be done would actually be accomplished. He would be the moderator in the decision-making process, and would have the final word in resolving any questions that might arise. Since that time, Keith has been our main spokesman. None of us has ever had reason to regret that decision.

For a brief period afterward there was some reaction. Some from outside the group accused us of having formally become a denomination with this step. However, the same accusation was made by the same people before this decision. On the other hand, a few of the pastors who were present throughout the process hoped for a more clearly defined authority, someone who would organize things in a more detailed way and hand down specific instructions to the rest. This had never been our way of operating, and it was made clear right away that our relationships would continue to be largely spontaneous.

On the whole, things moved along much more smoothly and efficiently after that. Keith is an excellent liaison man among us, self-effacing and completely honest. I've never heard a single accusation against him as self-seeking. But neither can he be accused of duplicity. While being very gracious, he has a sense of moral rightness and a touch of the Holy Spirit that makes him keen and clear in dealing with others. Once, when he and I were together in New Jersey for a ministers' conference, the brothers gave him the nickname of the "soft knife."

GROWTH IN FLORES

Naturally, the clearer definition of our relationships was a means to an end and not the end itself. The sense was growing in us all that we must put our hands to the task before us in a more effective and further-reaching way than we had before. For a year and a half we had been unavoidably preoccupied with internal problems. But now that the atmosphere was much clearer, we must move ahead.

The weekly Bible studies we were doing became more effective. Keith suggested that one or another take specific responsibilities in coordinating a series of studies, or in drafting the final conclusions for the printer. Besides the Wednesday morning sessions for prayer and study, we were also meeting on Monday nights with a larger group of church leaders, and for several months, most of those sessions were given over to dissertations based on the Wednesday Bible studies. A different pastor each week would be responsible for preparing the ministry.

Jorge and Ivan were seeing significant numerical growth in their united congregation meeting in the Flores district. During the first year after merging their two groups they had grown more than 50%. This was due to the dynamic evangelistic witness of the various home groups, and in no way was it the product of any kind of special emphasis or activity. Ivan was firmly convinced that any group would experience spontaneous and continuous growth if certain conditions prevailed: a close walk with the Lord, a proper relationship with one's fellow Christians, and an adequate sense of personal responsibility within the community.

One day Ivan and I had lunch together and I asked him to share with me the specific issues which he felt were the keys to this kind of church growth. As he did so, the conviction was born in me that the rest of the pastors and all the leaders of the various home groups related to our different congregations needed to hear these things. I encouraged Ivan to develop these thoughts and put them together in an orderly fashion and then plan to share them with the rest. The result was a series of conferences in August with nearly sixty men present. I don't think any of us had ever seen Ivan more anointed or with greater liberty than in those sessions when he shared with us the "cream" of his own experiences in making disciples in his home. God had fashioned and filled a vessel which was now pouring out the contents into other eager vessels.

CONCENTRATING ON OUR HOMEWORK

"And day by day continuing with one mind in the temple, and breaking bread from house to house, they were taking their meals together with gladness and sincerity of heart, praising God, and having favor with all the people. And the Lord was adding to their number day by day those who were being saved."

— Acts 2:46, 47

The conference in August, 1975 marked the first time that all the pastors in the group had a retreat with all their first-line men. Each of us chose from his own congregation the men that were bearing the load of pastoral responsibility along with us. These were all men who were leading small groups regularly in their own homes. Since all of them held secular jobs, we chose a weekend (Friday night through Sunday noon) and made reservations at the retreat center in Jose C. Paz.

The principal motivation for this retreat was the desire to make adjustments in a situation that could become a problem in the merging of different congregations. We could foresee the possibility of difficulties in bringing the groups together, since some of the groups — notably the one meeting in Flores — had strong, active and growing home meetings. But other congregations were still experimenting and had not yet come up with a pattern that was producing significant results. Because of this, these groups were more dependent upon their pastor and the larger church meetings. We felt that if this situation were not adjusted before merger, some of the Christians in those groups would suffer disorientation and a sense of disconnection from their pastor. In the end, the pastor would suffer as well and could even lose some of his sheep.

We certainly did not want any of the pastors to feel threatened. A merger, to be effective, had to be seen as a step forward, not backward. So it was essential that all the different congregations understand in practical ways the why-and-how of the shift over to delegation of most of the pastoral responsibilities and functions to home leaders and home meetings. Clearly, the one among us who had been most effective in this shift was Ivan Baker.

Practically all the ministry during the weekend was carried by Ivan, except for a message I was asked to give the group on the subject of "The Character of a Man of God." Ivan was masterful throughout the conferences. He had prepared his material well and he completely captured the attention of his audience. The timing was just right also. Everyone in the group had enough experience in working with others in a home setting to realize that not all is "peaches and cream," but they also saw the tremendous potential of this very effective alternative in pastoral care. Ivan put the whole scene into focus and gave us a charge we would never forget.

CHURCH HALLS OR PRIVATE HOMES

He began by pointing out the priority that we needed to give to the home as the natural and obvious place of birth and growth in the Christian life. Apart from the Jewish temple or synagogue it seemed to be the only place of regular meeting in the early church. Indeed, nothing is mentioned as to special buildings of any kind for the meetings of the church during the first three hundred years of its existence. Ivan pressed the point: "By meeting in the homes, or all together in one large place, the early church was able to maintain its essential unity. Nowadays, many church meetings and activities, based principally upon a temple or special hall, tend to divide, rather than unite God's people." To substantiate this, he suggested the following reasons:

— "The hall is too small for all the believers in a given area to meet in; yet it's so much larger than a home that the intimacy is lost.

— "It tends to underline our sectarian differences by drawing the lines of separation between one group and another in a nearly permanent fashion. It promotes a particular and localized identity, which tends to foment a protective, defensive, and possessive stance.

— "It focuses the attention, the work, and the funds of a Christian community in an inward and material direction, rather than in an upward, outward, and spiritual direction."

With quick references to the book of Acts and several epistles of Paul, Ivan illustrated the fact that the first Christians carried out in their homes many of the functions that today are relegated exclusively to temples and church buildings by the vast majority of Christians: preaching and teaching (Acts 5:42), the Lord's supper (Acts 2:46) and the community life of the church (Phil. 2; Rom. 16:5; I Cor. 16:19; Col. 4:15). He then ennumerated four reasons why he felt that the church as a whole must return to the homes for the bulk of its ministry:

1) "It is the ideal place to invite new Christians (or those who are open to the Gospel), to form them into effective disciples of Christ and to initiate them in Christian work and service. There is no better place than the home for evangelism, spiritual rebirth, exhortation, teaching, prayer, fellowship, and learning to function as a Christian.

2) "It is the place that offers the most possibilities for continued growth and multiplication. For one thing, about every five or six people have a home. This means that, as the

community grows, so do the number of possible meeting places where evangelism and training can take place. Thus, there will never be a lack of facilities, no matter how large or how fast the growth. When a work is begun with expensive or strange elements which few possess, the possibility of extension in ever-widening circles is greatly reduced. Exactly the opposite is the case when the work is dependent from the beginning upon elements which are within the reach of all. Each one who trains another must be able to say eventually, 'Now you do with others exactly as I have done with you.'

3) "In spite of all the advantages which the home offers as an ideal meeting place — kitchen, bathroom, one or two extra rooms for private prayer or consultation — no extra expenses are incurred. And the multiplicity of homes available — in varied geographical locations and at various social levels — make this an unexcelled instrument for unlimited growth.

4) "The size of the home obliges the community to function in relatively small groups. When one group grows in number they find themselves pressed for space. Then, instead of looking for a larger place, they simply divide into two homes. This expansion by dividing serves a double function: while opening new centers for growth and fellowship, new workers are developed to handle these responsibilities."

HOW DO THEY FUNCTION?

When this kind of program is projected with faith and vision, there is no limit to the possibilities for growth. But possibility and reality are two different things. So Ivan then took us into some of the more practical details of the functioning of the house groups:

"The very first step, he said, was for each Christian couple to dedicate their home to the Lord. This should be a specific act of faith in laying the home, and the lives of all those in the home, in the Lord's hand for the outworking of his sovereign will. This implies a clear dependence upon the Holy Spirit and the cultivation of a spiritual sensitivity in order to discern how and where He is working, so as to cooperate with Him. The development of a dynamic testimony in the home is not the result of carefully laid plans nor of intense activity. 'Except the Lord build the house, they labor in vain that build it.' Therefore, faith and simple obedience become the all-essential elements of fruitfulness.

"This disposition of the home will result in a new attitude toward one's neighbors and other regular contacts. He will seek to use existing natural bridges to develop these contacts: proximity, common interests, business contacts, family ties, work or school friendships, etc. And as each new person is won to the Lord, he is seen as the key to a whole new network of natural contacts. The first point of this new network is the immediate family of the new disciple: 'you and your house.' The opening of one's home is the first step in a new vision of the Christian community. We should keep in mind that Paul often spoke of 'the church in your house.' The home is now seen as an integral step in the expansion of the kingdom of God."

INFORMAL ENCOUNTERS

Ivan continued: "As interest among the neighbors and contacts grows and is nourished, the Lord will bless and some will be converted. There is no strict rule to follow here, but faith, prayer and a consistent witness will eventually bear fruit. This brings us to the second step.

"The most natural thing to expect of these new converts is that they will want to spend time with the person that led them to the Lord. They will have questions, problems, confessions, burdens, etc. They need to be prayed with, counselled specifically, instructed from the Word of God. Again, the most obvious setting for this is the home of the person who won them. With only one or two new converts, this is not much of a problem. But as the number grows, it will prove impossible to give them all unlimited individual time."

Ivan suggested that at that point it is adviseable to begin a regular weekly encounter with all these new ones together, in the home of the person who has won and is instructing them: "Again, this is not simply a mechanical procedure. This step is taken in an easy, natural way. Our tendency to rush ahead would only abort things at this point; we must give way to patience, faith, and constant prayer."

Ivan felt it was important to underline, as a practical measure, that this is merely an intermediate step: "This weekly encounter could not be properly called 'the church in the home.' It is, however, a very necessary stage where the couple in whose home these things are occurring is learning to handle greater responsibilities; yet they are not carrying the load all alone. In the meantime they continue to function as members of another home group and are thus under spiritual supervision. It is this relationship which provides the context and gives overall strength to their witness among their friends and neighbors.

"The orientation of their own immediate shepherd will help them to determine how best to handle problems and instruct those they have won to the Lord, but it is most important that they do this work themselves. They will surely make some mistakes, but their own growth in maturity and responsibility will far outweigh the few negative elements. They will be wise to limit their teaching and counselling to areas covered by their own experience."

STABLE HOME GROUPS

"It is possible that some will not progress

beyond this stage," Ivan counselled us. "Their own weekly encounters in their home will continue to bear a dependent relationship toward the home group where they are being shepherded. But it is most important that we not presume this limitation ahead of time. For in the vast majority of cases the most likely thing that will happen is that this smaller group will — possibly after some difficult initial testing times — continue to grow and reach others. Some, or all, of these will by now have become participants also in the group where their leader has been functioning as a faithful disciple."

The third step in Ivan's program for moving toward the church in the home, is the establishing of a stable group in the home where the couple has won a number to the Lord and has been nourishing them for a while in the faith and with prayer: "This third step would probably not be taken until the couple in question has a group of perhaps five to ten people under their immediate responsibility. But another requisite is equally important: the leading couple should evidence spiritual stability. This is seen in the phrase Paul used in writing to Timothy: '... faithful men, who will be able to teach others also.' In most cases, the growth of the group they have been leading will be evidence of their own firm position in the Lord.

"It may help," Ivan suggested, "to quickly review the main reasons for deciding at this point to separate this small group into another home meeting. Perhaps the strongest is what we could call spiritual paternity. All that are now leaving Group A to form Group B have been won by the emerging leaders or by some of these newly converted. In assuming the responsibility of shepherding them, the leaders have the most important qualification: that of paternity, or fatherhood; they are their spiritual parents. And although this is a new step, it is not entirely new; for the same leaders have been responsible until now for the major part of their spiritual growth and development.

"This third stage is a very significant step forward in the whole process, and is cause for genuine rejoicing. Through this step one of the more immediate goals of the original group has been reached. Some who were won to the Lord in the first group have now grown to the level of assuming a very important responsibility. They will now be immediately concerned to see growth and expansion in the newly formed group in their own home. This will motivate them to pray, plan, study, work with others, and develop some of their new disciples so as to bear future responsibilities in a similar way."

FAITHFULNESS IN SMALL THINGS

One item remained on Ivan's agenda for the retreat. He felt it necessary to outline certain principles regarding multiplication and growth of the home groups. He stated the basic theorum this way: "If each one does a little and is constant in this, together all of us will do a lot. This is a simple but most important principle. Church growth does not depend upon experts; rather it is dependent upon the effective division and delegation of responsibilities among the many who confess the lordship of Christ. Simple obedience to the Lord in bearing these responsibilities is far more important than any feelings of being qualified or having special gifts. We must not allow a sense of inferiority to keep us from doing what the Lord has commanded us. Faithfulness in the small things is a key to growth in maturity." Ivan emphasized the need to be constant in prayer, constant in witnessing, constant in faith. It is this constancy that makes one capable, agile, exemplary.

One of his recurring themes was the need for qualified workers. And he pointed out that this process of multiplication in the homes is the ideal setting for the multiplication of workers. Continuous growth is impossible apart from the formation of capable and willing workers.

Besides illustrating his basic thesis with many cases from his own wide experience, he gave us an apt illustration from nature. During mating season birds make their nests, lay a few eggs and sit on them until they hatch. Then the little ones are cared for until their feathers appear. Once covered with feathers, they are put out of the nest and learn to fend for themselves. All this is done in the simplest of circumstances. Ivan pointed out the disadvantages of systems and processes in the church which require special courses of training, or elaborate and sophisticated equipment. All of us must become reproductive; all must make disciples; all must bear fruit.

A FRESH START

Most of us who were present for the retreat were deeply moved and felt the whole picture had been so adequately presented that inaction on our part would be inexcuseable. I'm sure that many, like myself, returned home with a determination to review all that we were doing in the light of the truth presented to us during those days. My wife and I decided to apply these lessons just as they had been given. To our great joy, we found they were both practical and fruitful.

Although we had conducted many meetings in our home over the years, we were not satisfied with the fruit. For all the effort put forth, we felt the results were not very convincing. Now we began again, this time directing our attention specifically toward several people to whom we had been witnessing. One was an elderly lady who lived about ten blocks from our home. Another was a girl of 23 who had some personality problems. She too lived near us and we had been in touch with the family on various occasions since a relative had urged them to ask our help and prayers.

Another couple not far away we had befriended when the wife was quite ill in the hospital. I had since visited the home on several occasions and had witnessed to other members of the family. While they showed interest, they had not yet made any decision to clearly commit themselves to Christ.

Shortly after the retreat I contacted them all, one by one, to see if they had any interest in coming to a weekly gathering in our home for Bible study and prayer. To my surprise, everyone was pleased with the plan. So for months we met with them regularly every Thursday afternoon, going through the Scriptures, answering their questions, praying with them. After more than a year, they all made their decision, one by one, to surrender to Christ and follow him in baptism. By this time, the man's sister and mother had also decided to be baptized. My wife and I were overjoyed when we saw the six of them turn their lives over to the Lord. Although we moved from the neighborhood shortly thereafter, we have continued to have contact with them. Their faith has sustained them through some very difficult trials.

In the new area we moved into we began working in a similar way, with even greater fruitfulness. Here we started meeting with several new Christians that we had recently won to the Lord. Soon they were wining others. Within a year, one of the couples had won so many that we encouraged them to take the little flock into their own home. As I have continued to oversee them, they have matured and the group in their home is constantly growing. Our own home group is also growing. The same sort of thing is happening in homes all over Greater Buenos Aires. At this writing nearly a hundred groups are functioning in this way, many of which are second- and third-generation offspring.

Throughout the process we constantly keep before the disciples the essential unity of the Body of Christ as well as the importance of keeping the fires of testimony bright in reaching those without Christ. This aids in keeping the groups turned outward in evangelism. With the inflow of new life they avoid the problems that accompany a group that becomes ingrown. And by keeping in mind that all the Lord's children are our brothers and our sisters, they see themselves as an integral part of a vast community that covers the earth.

18

MERGERS IN THE METROPOLIS

"For a child will be born to us, a son will be given to us; and the government will rest on His shoulders ... There will be no end to the increase of His government or of peace ... The zeal of the Lord of hosts will accomplish this."

— Isaiah 9:6, 7

For nearly a year Angel Negro and I had been moving toward a merger of the two congregations we were pastoring. His was in José Ingenieros and mine in Villa Ballester, both areas being part of the northwestern suburbs of Buenos Aires. The group in Jose Ingenieros had begun many years before as a mission from a Plymouth Brethren assembly in the Capital. Over the years Angel had developed into one of the leaders, beginning as one of the more active and gifted evangelists and preachers among the youth. For a time he had been closely associated with Jorge Himitian when both were part of an interdenominational evangelistic team, preaching in the plazas and on the streets. Angel had also studied nights for several years at a Bible school in the city of Buenos Aires.

In 1967, three years after he was married to a daughter of one of the elders, both Angel and his wife Elisa were baptized in the Holy Spirit. They subsequently experienced many changes in their lives, as well as in the ministry in their congregation. At the time, he was working on the assembly line of a large automobile factory. However, the following year the brothers urged him to leave his secular employment and occupy himself full-time with the ministry of the Word. This step enabled him to respond to the many invitations that were coming from towns in the interior. His ancient Jeep was almost on its last leg, so the pastors pitched in and helped him exchange it for a later model Fiat automobile.

As he assumed the major responsibilities of pastoring the local assembly, God began to honor his faith and, within a brief time, most of the people were filled with the Holy Spirit and their meetings were filled with praise. While Angel has never made any pretense of being profoundly theological, he communicates exceptionally well with his audience. His earthy illustrations and intimate understanding of the mores of the people have made him a popular conference speaker.

Our congregation in Villa Ballester began in 1968, largely as a result of the concern of several families who had been disfellowshiped for departure from their church traditions. One of the families opened their home and we began meetings. By the end of the year the living room was jammed with earnest worshippers and seekers every Sunday evening, overflowing into the adjacent garage and the hall leading to the rear of the house. The following year we added a large hall at the back of the house with access from the street through the garage. Not a very fancy entrance, but it didn't matter, for the glory of the Lord was in the place!

Many were saved and scores were filled with the Spirit in the following months, as we grew together with the extending outpouring of the Holy Spirit throughout the country. From the very beginning the congregation was strongly family-oriented, being composed largely of complete families. So we had folk of all ages. Many young couples were incorporated into the congregation, with the result that we've always had an abundance of babies, toddlers, and howlers!

PUTTING IT TOGETHER IN SAN MARTIN

In mid-1974 Angel and I began serious

conversations about the possibility of merging our two congregations into one. Everything began to fall into place in quick succession. The county-seat of San Martin seemed to be the logical place to meet since it was about an equal distance from Villa Ballester and Jose Ingenieros. It was certainly more important as a commercial and industrial center than either of the others, and public transportation was excellent from all points.

At the same time my wife and I were looking for property for a home and the congregation in Villa Ballester had to move as well. Somewhat frustrated by our futile search for weeks, one day we decided to pool our resources and look for property that would serve the dual purpose of a meeting place and a home. The very next day Angel phoned to tell me he had found an interesting piece of property which was very well situated in the heart of San Martin! The price was lower than what we had expected to have to pay, and in short order we closed the deal.

Soon afterwards Angel suggested that he and his wife might be interested in building with us if we were open to the idea. It seemed too good to be true! So our architect began drawing up plans for a hall on the ground floor and two apartments above, each on its own floor. Eventually, another floor was added to the plan and construction got under way.

Delays in the building progress, however, seemed to be unnecessarily postponing the merger of the two groups. We had been having occasional united gatherings and they had gone very well. Everyone seemed enthusiastic about the prospect of a final and definite union. Eventually, the folk in José Ingenieros made the decision to join us in Villa Ballester until we could together make the move to San Martin. The knot was tied in October, 1975, and we've never had a single regret! Angel and I had always worked well together, and now our people and home leaders were getting acquainted and things were going quite smoothly. Another distinct advantage was that now Angel and I were both somewhat freer to engage in occasional itinerant ministry. Both of us felt the added strength of the other in working together and in handling problems or making decisions affecting the work in general.

FURTHER REGROUPING

In November the pastors planned a weekend retreat which would include pastors, home meeting leaders and all the wives from the Greater Buenos Aires area. I was asked to minister on the general subject of the prophetic gift. From the outset the Lord set his blessing on the gathering. The prayers, the flow in worship, the prophetic utterances given by many of those present, combined with the teaching sessions in a most beautiful manner. There was a charismatic flow among us all that was wonderful to behold. The entire retreat had the effect of a glorious refreshing among all that attended.

Then, between Christmas and New Year's Day the pastors and their families got together for a four-day mini-vacation (being summertime in Argentina). One afternoon as we relaxed near the swimming pool, Jorge shared with us a concern that had burdened his heart. Basically, his feeling was that our present grouping in different congregations scattered over the metropolitan area didn't fit the biblical pattern. In the Scriptures the meetings of the church as God's people seemed to have principally two valid expressions: (1) all together in one place, as the community of the redeemed, with no distinctions between them; and (2) small groups — relatively speaking — in the homes, mainly for fellowhip, study, prayer, mutual help and edification.

Jorge contended that our grouping into

different congregations was strictly a measure for convenience or to express preference, and did not contribute substantially to our spiritual unity. He urged us to be more open to the working of the Holy Spirit among us and to be obedient to his promptings. He said, too, that many were watching us to see whether we were really going to get together, or whether we would continue to be separate.

The size of our megalopolis continued to be a major problem, but at this point there really was not any insistence that we should try to get everyone in the area into a single congregation. Most of us had acknowledged that such an idea was rather unrealistic. What was expressed as the legitimate concern of most of the group was that we should not accept the present groupings of our various congregations as the final word; we should continue to be open for further moves toward outward expressions of our inward unity.

Even after suspending the large Monday night gatherings back in 1970, we continued to have occasional united gatherings when the believers from all over Greater Buenos Aires would come together. At these times the cooperating pastors would suspend their congregational activities and encourage all to participate. For a year or so we met one Sunday a month in a large gymnasium of a Catholic school in a central location in Buenos Aires.

Later we shifted over to a Sunday meeting every two months at the Ward College gymnasium in the western suburbs. But for the last several years, due to growth in the number attending, we have had to find larger quarters. We occasionally use a large theater or, if the weather is warmer, we sometimes use a soccer field and stadium. Often in the summer months we will meet together in a large park, adding a picnic and fellowship to the united meeting.

Each year at Easter we have a three-day series of conferences beginning on Good Friday.

Often Christians and church leaders come from great distances to share that weekend with us. And for several years we have had large annual retreats in April or May, usually held at a government hotel complex in the province of Cordoba, some fifteen hours from Buenos Aires in the geographical center of the country.

Still we realized that such occasional gatherings — important and vital as they have proved to be — are not an altogether adequate experience of our unity in Christ. Something more frequent and more intimate was needed.

As a practical and experimental plan of action, together we determined to look further into the possibility of regrouping and merging in terms of more or less clearly defined zones. Although we don't have any real problem over the fact that these situations sometimes overlap, nor in recognizing that there may be valid and overriding reasons why some Christians would meet with a community beyond the periphery of the zone where they live, we did feel that it would be best to tend toward some kind of geographical regrouping, because of the many advantages it offers. Logically, if a family can manage things in such a way as to live, work, study, fellowship and evangelize, mostly within a given area, life in general is going to be easier and more profitable. When our various activities are scattered over a vast area, we tend to run off in all directions at once, with the consequent frustration and lack of an overall sense of integration so prevalent in today's huge metropolitan areas.

These principles especially acquire validity and weight as the work expands and grows in number. When the number of disciples is small and scattered, it is often necessary to make significant sacrifices in terms of distance and time, just to meet together for fellowship. But when the kingdom of God begins to make wide inroads into many levels and areas of a metropolis, such sacrifices become somewhat redundant, and we need to be more realistic in facing the need for workable rearrangements. A valid answer for some is to move their household so as to be closer to the community where the integration is occuring.

GENTLE NUDGINGS OF THE SPIRIT

As we looked over our different situations and existing relationships, in general terms we decided that it would be well for us to work toward regrouping in four broad zones. These could be roughly defined as the capital city of Buenos Aires, the northern suburbs, the western suburbs, and the southern suburbs. Two of the pastors had people in their congregations from three of these areas, and several had folk in two of the prescribed zones. No matter. Our purpose was not to impose upon anyone an authoritarian decision from above that would prohibit him from commuting to another area for fellowship. We did feel, however, that if we were open in our hearts to the gentle nudgings of the Holy Spirit, in time a lot of these incongruencies would be easily adjusted. This has proven so far to be the case.

One of the pastors decided to merge with Jorge and Ivan. His people were already disposed for the step and were simply awaiting a decision on the part of the pastors. Another pastor began conversations with Angel and me over uniting with us in San Martin. Over the following months several in the southern suburbs began to draw closer to Keith who had moved to that area a couple years earlier. Eventually, things began to come together in the western suburbs as well, and several pastors in that broad area began steps toward merger.

We are still in the process, and it may well be unending. For, in reality, we can never properly say, "That's far enough." God is bringing his people together, and their united witness is producing a harvest. Who is to say where the horizon ends? "There will be no end to the increase of His government."

As we have moved forward together, we have sought valid ways of working out in practice our deep convictions concerning the unity of the church. Clearly, we have made mistakes and we have sometimes felt disoriented, but the basic conviction abides and is steadily deepening, born along by the continuing witness of the Holy Spirit, both in our hearts and in the circumstances before us.

We have learned patience, learned to await God's timing, learned to trust in his faithfulness. In the process we have learned that you don't just put things together mechanically and then watch them work. People can't be programmed like machines. Life is more important than activity. The building of the church of Jesus Christ is not a question of intricate clockwork. A moral and spiritual foundation and framework is absolutely essential.

19

A MORAL FRAMEWORK

"He who conceals his transgressions will not prosper, but he who confesses and forsakes them will find compassion."

— Proverbs 28:13

In college days one of the chapel speakers who most deeply affected my thinking was a lifetime missionary in China and Taiwan, Dr. James Graham. I shall never forget a charge he gave one day to the student preachers: "You must never cease to preach four things: — he said —

The exceeding holiness of God,

the exceeding sinfulness of sin,

the exceeding blessedness of the reward, and

the exceeding dreadfulness of the penalty."

His dissertations on the holiness and righteousness of God drove the roots of moral and spiritual integrity deep into the lives of many students.

God fully intends for His people to have a reverent fear of Him. Says Solomon the wise man: "The fear of the Lord is the beginning of wisdom." When indifference and moral laxity make inroads into the church, the Holy Spirit is grieved and often withdraws His blessing and the sweet sense of His presence. Issues become clouded and confused and the Word of the Lord no longer makes us tremble.

A spiritual awakening, if it is to continue, must bring again into the congregation of the faithful a holy fear of God, a longing for a life that pleases God, a hatred of iniquity. Genuine revivals, throughout the history of salvation, begin with repentance and heart-searching. They continue with sincerity, honesty and confession of all wrong. We must learn to keep short accounts with God. If we become lax in order to save embarrassment, if we close our eyes to sin in order to spare an unwelcome scene, if we allow ourselves to minimize moral issues while maximizing the intensity of religious activity, we may be sure that our sin will find us out. The sharp edge of spiritual discernment will be dulled, the Word of God will no longer find in us a ready response, and the fellowship of the faithful will become a drag.

We have discovered that nothing is more distasteful than to have to deal with immorality, either in ourselves or in others. Whether dishonesty and lying, or thievery, or adultery, there is a natural dread in us that makes us prefer to bury our heads in the sand, or wash our hands of the whole nasty affair.

We have seen glorious and promising spiritual awakenings go bad through coverup of moral misconduct. We have seen intimate colleagues destroy their own families or make total shipwreck of outstanding ministries by failing to watch out for those things that dishonor God. The breakdown is gradual, but eventually the bottom is reached. The Holy Spirit is grieved, the offender lies under the heavy burden of a guilty conscience, and often many others are wounded as well.

The Gospel of God's grace is the only effective remedy for these cases. Our Lord is full of mercy and forgiveness, reaching out to us in our need, magnifying the greatness of His love and the infinite value of Christ's death on Calvary. Yet His grace is not cheap; it is not a band-aid or a sugar-coated pill. It comes freely to the contrite in spirit, to the humble and repentant. But God sits in judgment upon the haughty, the proud, the self-sufficient.

DISCREPANCIES RESOLVED

In a society like ours where moral laxity and

spiritual mediocrity have become the order of the day, it takes great strength of conviction to simply stand firm in the knowledge that God is righteous in His judgment upon our social and moral disorder. But He has called the church to do more than just say "Amen" to the Word of the Lord. Peter tells us that judgment begins with the house of God. Jesus said that His disciples were to be light in the darkness, leaven in the loaf, and salt in the world. The people of God have always been called to illustrate to the world around how much better it is for all concerned if we live in the center of His Will. The church is God's answer to the world's need, God's alternative to our disintegrating social order.

There was a time, not more than a few years back, when most of us who are working together in the pastorate in Buenos Aires, had some fairly fuzzy thinking about these matters. Not in principle, but in practice. We could have all said a hearty "Amen" to the above paragraphs, but when we got right down to the line, it was difficult to stand firm. Part of the problem was probably some sense of impotence; we wanted to see those who were bound set free, but we didn't know quite how to liberate them. Therefore, we tended to be lax with them. Their conscience was not helped, and neither was the church's sense of reverence for God's ways. Over the years the falacies of such a loose position began to convince us there had to be a better way.

But what a difference there has been — in both conviction and in results — since we began to seriously study together the Word of the Lord on these different issues. In 1974 we began studying in earnest one day every week the various prevailing moral problems that characterize our society. And one by one we came to see "eye to eye," where in the past there had been wide discrepancies. Then in a series of sudies in 1975 and 1976 under the general heading of "Relationships between Christian brothers," we delved into Scriptural teaching concerning how we were to deal with sin, in ourselves and in our brethren. This took us into a thorough-going Bible study on discipline in the church, and the whole moral issue began to come clearly into focus. No longer were we fumbling in the dusk; we knew where we were to stand and what we were to do, and we were thoroughly united.

After this we began to see really remarkable recoveries in those who had long been homosexuals, adulterers, irate, liars, thieves, etc. With a strong orientation on the felicity and the sacredness of the home in God's order; with a solid basis and expression of spiritual unity among the Christians in the community; with an awareness among all of the need for a wholesome life and a clean moral character; with the conviction that we must all stand together to help and to recover the straying sheep; the kind of atmosphere is present which is conducive to recovery, forgiveness, reorientation and — where necessary — excommunication.

Basically, the procedure we have followed in dealing with cases of recurring moral iniquity is to deal, first of all, with the offender in private. He is exhorted to repent, confess and totally abandon all sinful actions and attitudes. Where others have been involved, confession and restitution is necessary, even to the point of public confession before the church where the saints have been scandalized by the misdeeds of one of their number. I could hardly have believed, years ago, that these very biblical methods, when carried through in humility, could effect such healing, could bring out the compassion in the hearts of God's people, could so completely enfold those who are repentant.

EFFECTS OF DISCIPLINE

An unforgettable scene is written on the

memory of my mind, in which a man came forward to confess a horrible sin. His repentance and humility were evident, his confession clear (without any unbecoming details), his needs for forgiveness and restoration manifest. The saints were stunned and then moved to compassion. Several told me afterwards, that they were acutely aware that, but for the grace of God, they could have been in the same place. When the confession was over, those who cared to do so were invited to gather around the man and his wife. What heartfelt prayers were lifted to the throne of grace! What tears of humiliation were shed! What a sense of mutual dependence upon each other and upon the Lord was evident! "Where sin abounds, grace does much more abound."

In another case, the offender — a homosexual — was deeply sorrowful, but confessed he was unable to conquer his inordinate passions. He was brought before the community (without any visitors present) and reminded of the grave consequences of continuing in his sin. A brother was assigned to him to pray and counsel with him until he was free. In the meantime the rest of the saints were not to fellowhip with him. He must suffer ostracism for his wrong. For years he had been helpless to overcome, and his former pastor had all but given up on him. But never before had he been brought before the community to be dealt with in this manner. Within a few months he was a totally changed man, completely free from this besetting sin. His countenance changed remarkably. He testified that it was the discipline of the saints — their firm commitment to see him set free — that effected the change.

In every case of discipline, we keep in mind that the goal before us is always complete recovery and reinstatement within the family of the faithful. The discipline is never for punitive purposes, but corrective in nature. The results have been far more effective and satisfactory than anything we have ever witnessed before. The community learns to live in the light, to keep short accounts, and to keep the lines of fellowship open. But when an offense occurs, the entire community is moved to compassion and, if necessary, to united action, in order to see the straying one restored.

While most of the cases we have dealt with have brought forth clear evidence of repentance, occasionally we have had to push ahead in the face of a determination to continue in known sin. In one case a person who was reprimanded for living in adultery refused to break off the liaison. The individual was dealt with patiently and lovingly over a period of weeks. The pastor and his wife, and leading brothers and sisters in the congregation prayed, exhorted, and opened the scriptures with the offender; all to no avail.

Finally, the case was brought before the men of the community who are heads of families; a special prayer meeting was called to lift the matter in unison before the Lord; then the person was given another week to abandon the wrong. When it was clear that no change had taken place, the entire congregation concurred as the pastor announced to the party that the fellowship of the saints had been withdrawn and the person was left to his fate before the righteous Lord.

Perhaps the most significant facet of the entire process was the sense of unanimity in the congregation. It was a community decision; there was no arbitrary imposition of authority. The process took nearly four months and throughout this time no effort was spared to effect reconciliation.

THE BEAUTY OF HOLINESS

On Easter weekend each year we normally have a special series of three or four conferences which is a happy occasion when saints from all over Buenos Aires come together for large meetings in a central location. In 1977 Keith Bentson gave a series of messages at the annual conferences on the subject of the fear of God. The first message was on the fact that God is to be feared. The following one underlined the goodness and holiness of God's law. Then he dealt with the righteousness of God and the unrighteousness of man, and finally, how God transforms lives so as to be pleasing to Him.

Many came under conviction for a lighthearted attitude toward God and toward sin. At the conclusion of the final meeting there were a great many confessions as we bowed in prayer and humility before God. Then most of us turned to the person next to us and confessed our sins one to another and prayed for each other. The touch of God was upon the whole scene. Some Roman Catholic friends were present and remarked that they had never seen Protestants confess their sins to others like this. They realized now that the Catholics didn't have a corner on confession!

A couple weeks later we had a five-day national spiritual retreat in a government hotel complex in Córdoba province. For the main morning conferences we invited Dick Williams from Chicago. The remaining conferences were given by local men. We had made no suggestions to Williams concerning the subject of his ministry among us, but it perfectly coincided with all that the Lord had been emphasizing to us concerning moral integrity and holiness of life.

He talked about the value of solid moral and spiritual foundations, about the need to discover and confess the darkness in our lives and to destroy the strongholds built by sinful habits and defended by Satanic hosts. Again, there was a wide-spread sense of conviction of sin. During those days, and for weeks following, there was a lot of cleaning-up being done in hundreds of lives.

As confession was made and restitution effected where applicable, many Christians were delivered of long-standing problems of conscience. The bondage of sin was effectively broken and many entered into a liberty in their lives and their walk with God that they had never known before.

It is most unfortunate that too frequently the idea of a godly life and honorable character is associated with weakness, timidity, lack of willpower. God is interested that holiness and integrity be recognized as something beautiful, robust and worthwhile. In the Levitical priesthood of the Old Testament he had the priests clothed with beautiful embroidered garments of the finest linen. God's people were exhorted to "worship the Lord in the beauty of holiness." The moral fiber and strength of character of godly men and women were lauded and valued as something to be emulated among all the saints.

If Peter tells us that "judgment begins at the house of God," then clearly the Lord is seeking evidence and fruit of holiness and right conduct in the lives of His people. It's not a narrow-minded legalism that draws us into the presence of God; rather it is the beauty of His holiness, the glory of His grace, the assurance of His faithfulness and integrity. God is forming a people for Himself, of whom He is not ashamed to be called "their God." His grace and determined purpose — the "zeal of the Lord of hosts" — will surely accomplish this.

20

GROWING ROOM

"Behold, the farmer waits for the precious produce of the soil, being patient about it, until it gets the early and late rains."

— James 5:7

One of the factors that makes the produce of the soil precious is the patience necessary in order to see the harvest. Only the patient ones will continue to labor during the stage when the plant is sending down its roots.

Over the years time and again we expressed dissatisfaction with what seemed to be the traditional face of evangelical Christianity in Latin America. The fruit, the results, were hardly impressive. But if the observable results were not impressive, neither were our pet theories and our dreams. Therefore, a number of us resolved to stand together and plant and plow in faith until a harvest was forthcoming.

Whatever may yet be lacking — and we are very conscious of areas that need much enlightenment and development — we must confess that the difference in the fruit we have seen in recent years clearly and abundantly exceeds what we had known in earlier years. The quality of normal everyday living, the freshness of spontaneous outreach and witness, the informality and integrity of the groups growing together in the homes, the strength and understanding prevalent in the average family, the growing community spirit: these and other qualities were only longed-for items in the past; they are now present realities, giving us a great deal of hope for the church in the days ahead.

A NORMAL CHRISTIAN

Perhaps a couple brief case histories will

illustrate what I mean. Take Pablo, for instance. He had tried his hand in several business operations, but was only barely keeping his head above water. His marriage was sorely tested, due to his impulsiveness and unsuccessful ventures. The one child, a pre-schooler, was a bundle of nerves and frequently uncontrollable.

Then one day a client told him he needed Jesus Christ. He and his wife accompanied the client to a meeting and they liked what they saw and felt. Within a few weeks they both made a firm commitment to Christ and were soon baptized. Shortly thereafter they were filled with the Holy Spirit and began to testify to friends, neighbors, customers, and family. Within a few months, Pablo won to the Lord a customer, his own brother, the municipal inspector, and a family that lived across the street from his business.

One by one, they began to accompany him and his wife to the weekly meeting in another home. But from the first, Pablo knew it was his responsibility to visit and counsel those he had won. This made him diligent in prayer and obliged him in turn to seek counsel from the leader of the home group so as to be able to properly instruct his charges. Soon all these were baptized in water and filled with the Holy Spirit.

In the meantime Pablo continued to share his experience with others. He was also bringing other areas of his own life under the lordship of Christ. Encountering problems in the business, he would seek help and orientation, instead of impulsively resolving things as in the past. Before long, the business was prospering and he was able to begin construction of a home of his own.

Pablo was told early in his walk with the Lord that he would continue to be responsible for those he won, even though for a time they attended another meeting along with him. Within a reasonable period of time he would take this group of disciples into his own home for further orientation and growth. In this way, he would grow himself and develop more effective qualities of leadership. So about twelve months after having begun attending a home meeting himself, he started one in his own home. In short order, the group learned to pray and handle responsibilities and problems that developed among them. Pablo, in turn, was being counselled individually by the leader of the meeting he had been attending.

Pablo's group continued to grow. Soon he won another couple to the Lord. Then the couple who lived across the street from his business won another couple. And growth continues, both numerically and spiritually. They study and pray together. They care for the needs of each other. Together they take on projects that will draw out the different qualities of those composing the group. All the time Pablo is seeking to develop other leaders within the group, conscious that some of them will one day be caring for a similar flock in their own home.

As Pablo has matured he has become a part of the leadership in the congregation, sharing this responsibility with the other house leaders. Every two or three months they have a retreat together for intensified prayer and study and for review of the work of the church in general. These retreats are led by the pastors of the congregation who oversee the work as a whole, and who themselves also lead groups in their own homes.

Pablo's case is especially interesting because of the fact that he is typical of the average man-on-the-street that one finds on every hand. He has had no special theological training whatever. He didn't complete high school, and has no particular training for a trade. Yet he loves the Lord and has committed himself without reserve to him. Having put his hand to the plow, he determined to not look back. He governs his home well and his wife and children are happy and exemplary. His business acquaintances point him out as worthy of confidence and his fellow-Christians find him both understanding and compassionate. In a word, he is a normal Christian.

GOSPEL CHAIN REACTION

Another who found reality and stability in Christ was Alberto. One of his clients suggested that he visit a Christian camp in the province of Córdoba while away on vacation. Alberto and his wife were having problems and he had already decided that this would be their last trip together before separating. They thought they might stop in at the camp briefly, more out of curiosity than because of any great interest. Arriving at supper time, they joined the campers in the dining hall. Alberto's wife spotted a lady she recognized who turned out to be the wife of one of the pastors from Buenos Aires. Immediately they became absorbed in conversation. That night she attended the meeting and was deeply touched by the words of one of the hymns. She had never felt anything quite like it.

The following afternoon the pastor invited Alberto and his wife to accompany a group of the campers who planned to go to a nearby lake to swim and have a picnic. They accepted, but without any real enthusiasm. While in the water, a number of the fellows who had come along were sharing their faith and joy with Alberto, who began to open his heart. After a short while, Alberto asked to be baptized. His wife, looking on from the shore, was utterly amazed to see the group gathering around her husband and then dipping him into the water! That night they had quite a struggle between them over the issue, but the next day she also surrendered.

When they returned to their home in Buenos Aires, they kept in touch with the pastor who soon had them integrated in the group meeting in his home. Alberto and his wife started sharing their newly discovered peace and victory with relatives, neighbors and business acquaintances. Before long, several turned to Christ, and within three months the pastor had them all shifted over to Alberto's home for their regular weekly gatherings. Then the group really started to grow!

Alberto was another who never looked back. In spite of difficulties and nagging problems, he kept learning, praying, confessing and making restitution, but all the time giving witness to the goodness and mercy of the Lord. Within months their group grew to forty or fifty, including a vibrant bunch of young people. Whole families were converted. Several were good musicians and they began to compose choruses and set Scripture verses to music. As their joy sounded out in worship and song, still others were attracted. The small community became a beehive of activity.

Unable to confine the burgeoning group to their own home, they divided into two groups and continued growing. Before long, they divided again, and then again. Within two years, Alberto and his family had grown to nearly a hundred new and thriving Christians.

DEVELOPING LEADERS AND
BUILDING FAMILIES

And on and on they grow. Some that Alberto won to Christ are now leaders of home groups. Maturity and fruitfulness are the prime factors indicating future leaders. As these qualities become evident in the believers, they are singled out for special attention and encouragement, to see that they handle their responsibilities seriously and with faith, instead of viewing them as burdens.

Once a home group becomes stable and the

leader and his family show clear capability and a firm commitment to the larger community, gradually the leader is given increased responsibility before the entire congregation in such a way as to win the confidence of all. He is encouraged to exercise his gifts and grace with faith, but without pushing. He is part of a ministering team, working under the supervision of the pastors, sharing the burdens and the joys of all. Together they constitute a vital part of the great family of faith. Wherever they meet other Christians they treat them as brothers, no matter what label they wear. We sense that if we all do the job the Lord has assigned us, in sharing the Gospel with others and making disciples, and if we recognize that all Christians are part of the church of Jesus Christ, then we can keep the lines of communication and witness open so that the Holy Spirit can eventually bring us together in a valid catholic expression of the unity of God's people.

Earlier I referred to another facet that has given stability to the testimony as a whole: the fact that our witness is not simply to individuals, but to families. No matter what the first point of contact is, the saints are quick to take the glad tidings to the family nucleus. The newly converted are instructed to let their light shine before other members of the family and to exercise faith for their conversion. Before baptizing an individual, we normally seek to give ample opportunity to the family so that the significant step of baptism can be taken as a family group, if possible. Of course, this is consequent upon a clear confession of faith and commitment to Jesus Christ on the part of each person being baptized. But we have found that when our faith is projected from families to families, God honors that approach and many families have turned to the Lord together.

All of this has involved a lot of teaching and counsel for the families. Husband and wife relationships, child raising, effective communication between parents and their youth, family outings and projects, budgeting, home-making: all come under the scrutiny of the Word of God and the light of the Holy Spirit. Where there was darkness, now there is light; where there was conflict, now there is peace and understanding; where there was silence, now there is communication; where before all went separate ways, now they work and play together. Gradually, family life becomes the bright spot of the Christian's life, the focus for witness, the source of joy and the refuge from the world of struggle and tribulation around us. Children that were once nervous and burdensome to their parents, have become the object of their affection and tempered discipline. As these children grow into adolescence, instead of being lost to the world, they continue to be a vital part of the growing family, as well as of the Christian community.

The youth have become more diligent in their studies, more helpful and considerate in the home, more Christian in their approach to courtship and marriage. Their commitment to God and to the Christian community as well as to their own family constitute the heart of their daily life and their world view. Constant improvement, both in attitudes and work, in goals and in study, have taken the place of mediocrity and passivity.

THE JOB BEFORE US

In a certain sense we could say that our quest over the years has been to find an answer to the question: What are we saved for? What does salvation mean? The testimony of this book is indicative of the experience and understanding at which we have arrived thus far. We would be among the first to admit that the answer is not complete.

As we look realistically at the job yet to be

done, we are aware of needs in specific areas. One of the most satisfying rewards we have known as a group of pastors has been to see laymen emerging as capable leaders over growing flocks, gifted and stable men with exemplary families. Yet we want to see many of these promising men moving into fuller and broader ministry and responsibility in the church. We must be careful not to hinder their growth by standing in their way ourselves. Several who are presently **functioning as pastors** in our various communities came up 'through the ranks' in just this way. Among them are professionals, business men, and college professors, some of whom are now in the ministry full-time.

One of our projects is to give more attention to their theological education. Many of these men are diligent students, but recognize their need of mature guidance in this area. Aware that no one training program will fit every situation, we are experimenting with a variety of programs in the different communities. These include, variously, occasional seminars, regular classes which follow specific courses of study, personal study assignments and pastoral study programs. Gradually, we are getting these materials into print, but admit that the pace does not seem to be rapid or intensive enough.

Some of the pastors have been more fruitful than others. Some have a large measure of maturity and wisdom. Some have outstanding gifts and graces. They have a solid base and years of valuable experience. These men need to be moving in an enlarging circle. So we are seeking ways whereby their participation and ministry can achieve growth and edification among the Lord's people on a larger scale. Because they are much appreciated on the local scene and because they have put down roots where they are, it is not easy for them to move out into regions over the horizon. Yet the move is necessary and vital to the dynamic expansion of

Augusto Ericsson at the organ, 1979.

Author interpreting for Ern Baxter at Pastor's Retreat in 1980.

"ustedes son la luz de este mundo"

1980 Embalse Retreat.

1980 Embalse Retreat. Pastors rejoicing on the platform. From left Swindoll, Negro, Baker, Himitian, Vigilante.

Afternoon fellowship on veranda at the same Retreat.

Worshipping the Lord at the same Retreat. (Bentson on his knees.)

1981 photo of Argentine Pastors at the airport with Arthur Wallis (3rd from left) and Tony Morton (2nd from left) who had just arrived from England.

1982 — Worshipping together at Buenos Aires Retreat.

the kingdom of God.

We are experimenting with this kind of outreach in different ways, so as to discover an effective 'modus operandi' that satisfies and delivers the goods. One of our leading men in Buenos Aires moved to another large city in the interior of the country in 1981, primarily to work closely with a group of nearly twenty pastors in the city who represent different congregations. He is also giving oversight and ministry of an itinerant nature to nearby areas, as well as making regular bi-monthly visits to another city in a country just over the border.

Another of our principal leaders recently spent three months with his family in the capital city of another Latin American country, so as to help the pastors there coordinate an effective program of consolidation and outreach, including an intensive training program for emerging leaders. Others are making regular, and sometimes rather lengthy, visits for ministry and counselling to other cities and to all the countries that border on Argentina. We anticipate the possibility of some of the pastors eventually moving to other areas, for greater or lesser periods of time, as the developing situations seem to require in the future.

Perhaps it is redundant to say that we long to see more steady evangelistic growth. Some real gains have been made in this direction, but we are not yet seeing the entire community giving itself away in spontaneous and continuous witness. What we have seen in some is so encouraging that we long to see it in all.

We are concerned about having an effective witness in society at large. Knowing that we are to be a light in the darkness, and salt in the earth, we seek to be sensitive to areas of social need. For years several of the communities have made regular monthly contributions to several orphans' homes. On various occasions, fairly large groups of Christians have gone to one of the homes to do maintenance work and repairs, ladies in one community have woven scores of wool sweaters for the children, and school supplies have been purchased at the beginning of the school year for the orphans. Moreover, several of the families have adopted one or two orphans each.

Tons of goods and thousands of dollars have been donated by the churches in Buenos Aires to victims of flooding in northern Argentina, being distributed through pastors in the affected areas. Carloads of men have made lengthy trips at their own expense to help put up emergency housing, working day and night over long weekends. Most of the congregations in Buenos Aires have significantly helped the less privileged families to build their own dwellings, both with manual labor and with funds for the purchase of building materials. This is the only way that some of these families will ever have a home of their own.

Making disciples in the homes has been perhaps the major key in our unfolding experience of spiritual recovery over the past ten or twelve years. But we sense that this is only the beginning. Christian homes are the most essential key to growth in the days ahead. Therefore, we are expecting to see further developments and more effective orientation for the home groups and family evangelism. We feel sure that the face of the church of the future is going to look more like multiplied thousands of homes than like huge meetings or fancy buildings or ministerial 'superstars.'

We are also seeking ways to more effectively share with and embrace our brothers and sisters who do not completely agree with us and either feel no attraction to us or feel threatened by us. Like others we have made mistakes and have occasionally given vent to sectarian attitudes. But we recognize that the family of God is one. We have determined to "beat our swords into plowshares" and to stand together with all our brethren in Christ, insofar as it is possible. Ground has been recovered in this respect, and we have experienced sincere reconciliation with several from whom we had been formerly estranged. Yet we can hardly be satisfied until we are at peace with all our brethren.

God is giving his people growing room these days and wonderful changes are taking place. He has smiled upon us and made us recipients of His great grace. We fully believe that we shall continue to grow, continue to learn, to adapt, to mature. As long as we have breath, our story is unfinished. Luther said, "The church reformed is the church reforming." We could say as well, "The church renewed is the church renewing." There is no stopping place.

Therefore, in a very real sense, this is not the end. It's only the beginning . . .

21

EPILOGUE: OUR VISION AND FAITH

"And he said to them, "Please listen to this dream which I have had."

— Genesis 37:6

In the preface I said that this book was written as a response to some questions. I hope I have not disappointed my readers. Nonetheless, I'm sure there remain a number of unanswered questions and concerns. I confess that I have several myself. The same could be said of my colleagues in Buenos Aires.

Our experience in these things is still somewhat brief: about seventeen years. Obviously, this is too short a time to speak from a historical perspective. But we consider it is sufficient to be able to give a coherent testimony of the things we have experienced together . . . and continue to experience. What has been presented here is part of the heritage of our faith. We believe that the changes and adjustments we have lived through — both theological and practical — are significant enough to merit such a testimony, so that our Christian brothers and sisters might evaluate them and, perhaps, be enriched thereby. To draw any final conclusions would be premature.

Moreover, we are not unaware of the fact that the recounting of such recent events is charged with a certain unavoidable subjectivity. Every effort on the part of the reader to obviate such elements will be sincerely appreciated, so that the more objective elements might contribute to the enlargement and blessing of the church of Jesus Christ.

Humbly and sincerely, we believe that we have something of value to share in the present process of the church's restoration. And with deep conviction we recognize our need to receive from our brothers in different places that which they have received in their own experience of spiritual renewal.

We feel that it would not be strictly correct to catalog our experience under the heading of "charismatic movement." Certainly the charismatic experience, the fulness of the Holy Spirit, is a vital part of the total picture. We recognize that it especially served as a springboard to generate the process of spiritual renewal, but it would not seem to us to be the most outstanding characteristic of our common experience. The principal actors in the story just told, more than leaders of a spiritual movement, or theoretical reformers, are really just pastors of the flock of God. In accord with this sense of vocation, the principal focus of our concern is simply the church: her building and coordination, her renewal and restoration and, consequently, her mission in the world, that is to say, the evangelization of the nations. Our hearts burn with a passion to see in our days a great forward thrust in the divine process to restore the church to her place of glory and fulfillment of God's eternal purpose.

DOES THE CHURCH NEED RENEWAL?

It is a self-evident fact that today, in most of the world, and in most of the varied Christian groups and denominations, in a greater or lesser degree, there is a ferment of spiritual renewal. Our experience, in that sense, is by no means isolated or singular. We understand that the present world-wide outpouring of the Holy Spirit is a sovereign work of God who has Himself set in motion an irreversible process which is to issue in the restoration of the church.

Perhaps we should here propose an answer to the question: Why is the renewal or restoration of the church to be considered a necessity? Many seem to be satisfied with the present situation of the church; perhaps they would only sense a need for a greater evangelistic outreach. Others seem resigned to the prevailing mediocrity, and simply try to do the best they can under the circumstances. We want to state clearly that we are neither satisfied nor resigned. God Himself has challenged us. We have felt obliged to make significant changes in our faith and our expectation as to what the church is to be prior to the return of her Lord.

We no longer believe that the church will finish her race in the earth worn out, luke-warm and defeated. We cannot resign ourselves to accept the current situation as final. The church of Jesus Christ cannot finish up divided by thousands of human and denominational walls, without holiness, without power, without love among the brethren, without a vital commitment to our Lord. To us it goes without saying that the church needs refreshing and restoration. And not only is it needed; it's coming! More than that, it's already happening!

Restore means to revert things to the way they were at the beginning. We must return to the ancient foundation laid by Jesus Christ and his apostles. Saint Paul's words resound in our ears: "No man can lay a foundation other than the one which is laid . . ." (I Cor. 3:11); "If any man is preaching to you a gospel contrary to that which you received, let him be accursed" (Gal. 1:9). What he and the other apostles taught and proclaimed was the word of the Lord for every generation. Yet history has witnessed distortions, additions, tangents and detours throughout the centuries. Clearly, we must return to the beginning.

In reality, the church has been returning for several centuries. But since we have not yet arrived, we must continue to return. And this involves changes. We must be willing to leave

Pastors preparing to serve the Lord's Supper to 3500 at the Retreat in Buenos Aires in 1982.

Same Retreat. 3500 praising the Lord.

Same Retreat. Jorge Himitian preaching.

**1983 — Retreat in Buenos Aires.
Angel Negro preaching to 4000.**

Same Retreat. Preparing the Lord's Supper.

behind customs, practices and teaching that are not in accord with the apostolic orientation. Our common tendency is to hold onto our well-worn customs and religious traditions, and systematically resist every kind of change. I appeal to my readers to recognize the need for adjustments and be willing to seriously consider the changes suggested, seeking to honestly discern if these are from the Lord.

GOD'S UTOPIA

Jesus asked his Father that all those that believe in Him might be perfected in unity, so that the world might know and believe in Him (Jn. 17:21, 22). We believe that the Father will respond to his Son's request, and that the day will come when all His children will be perfected in unity here on earth, "that the world may believe." We believe, too, that this unity will be the culmination of a gradual integrating process under the direction of the Holy Spirit.

The apostle Paul declares in Ephesians 5:25-27 that Jesus Christ has purposed to purify and sanctify his church, in order that "He might present to Himself the church in all her glory, having no spot or wrinkle or any such thing." Moreover, he states in chapter 4:11-16 of the same epistle that Christ established in the church apostles, prophets, evangelists, pastors and teachers . . . "until we all attain to the unity of the faith, and of the knowledge of the Son of God, to a mature man, to the measure of the stature which belongs to the fulness of Christ."

What? "Until we all attain to the unity of the faith . . . to the measure of the stature which belongs to the fulness of Christ?" That sounds like a utopian dream! But . . . it's God's Utopia! If this were our program or our project, we might well expect that others would say, "Sounds like a beautiful ideal . . . but it's impossible!" But the one who has proposed to unite the church is GOD HIMSELF! Is there any way He can fail?

Jesus Christ has purposed to build the church and perfect it in order to present it to Himself holy and glorious. Does He not have all the grace and all the resources necessary to do the job? Inasmuch as we're dealing with God's purpose, obviously, it is not a utopian dream, since He has all the power in heaven and on earth to fulfill what He has purposed.

Our faith and hope is that the Lord is going to fulfill all His purpose in the renewal of the church. We cannot be satisfied with less than that, though the road before us be long and difficult. We are irrevocably committed to seeing all the children of God united in one body. A superficial fraternal relationship is not the answer. We fully understand that this is a process that only God can bring about; but we firmly believe that He will do it. For our part, we are ready to act in faith, to exercise patience, to unite with others, to obey God. We want to do all the Lord would have us to do.

According to Paul the divisions within the body of Christ are evidence of spiritual immaturity and lack of growth. But we believe the church is going to mature and grow up; the pastors, too, are going to mature. In the measure that that happens, we will abandon our sectarianism, and as mature Christians we will be able to express before the world our complete unity, not merely for a few days so as to have an evangelistic campaign after which everyone returns to his own corner, but rather as the body of Christ, as a single family or community, in each town, in every city.

AREAS FOR REVIEW

Finally, I want to suggest to my readers — and especially to pastors and other Christian leaders — an honest review of the experiences referred to in this book; an objective evaluation of the truths expounded therein; and a predisposition to assimilate all that is positive. As a beginning, I would mention several specific areas where the church, in general, could benefit from a spiritual renewal and a restoration of the testimony and experience of the early church:

A greater sensitivity to the sovereign moving of the Holy Spirit. The Spirit of God is the only one who is Sovereign in the house of God. We must not limit Him in His activity, in His work of conviction, in His distribution of gifts, in His choice of timing, in His methods or in His selection of human instrumentality. Let us learn to follow His leading, to hear His voice, to move under His inspiration. Let us draw near to God and cultivate a spiritual sensitivity. On occasion this will involve making room for something to which we are unaccustomed. Paul's exhortation is fitting here: "Do not quench the Spirit; do not despise prophetic utterances. But examine everything carefully; hold fast to that which is good" (I Thess. 5:19-21). The church should be always filled with the Holy Spirit; it should move under the anointing of the Spirit at all times.

A liturgical reformation. Many Christians are tired and bored with the traditional order of church services. To them the rites seem to be without spontaneity, lacking vitality and spiritual content. The experience of drawing near to God ought to move the deepest fibers in one's being. It should awaken hope and faith. It should provoke worship, wonder, humility. We should promote a more spontaneous participation from the entire congregation. There is no need to restrain expressions that combine the physical and the emotional with the spiritual, such as raising the hands, clapping, shedding tears, praying spontaneously, etc. All these manifestations have biblical antecedents. Let us give more place to songs of joy and to unprogrammed testimonies.

A rediscovery of the Gospel of the kingdom of God. The initial steps in the Christian life are of vital importance. If one begins "on the wrong foot," he will find it hard to add later those elements that should have been included at the beginning. A cheapened Gospel makes the subsequent task of spiritual edification very difficult. We must learn to start out properly. to start where Jesus Christ began, where the apostles began: with a vigorous Gospel message, a proclamation that opens hearts, that causes hope to be born, that generates faith, that provokes surrender and obedience to Christ. A good beginning — a genuine new birth — includes repentance, a renunciation of selfishness, a clear commitment to Christ as Lord, followed by baptism in water, the fulness of the Holy Spirit, and integration into the believing community. In this biblical frame of reference for the Gospel, the lordship of Jesus Christ is the outstanding element, and the government of God is the issue that gives coherence to the whole framework.

The focus on discipleship as a valid alternative for the work of pastoring, or shepherding. Today among pastors, priests and other church leaders there is wide-spread frustration with the classical methods of pastoral care. At all levels of growth — from the "newborn" to the veterans — there are losses and desertions from the faith. Many of the widely accepted methods in use today for evangelism and pastoral attention have little or nothing to do with that employed by our Lord. In order to carry out His purpose in building the lives of His followers, he created a **teacher-disciple relationship.** Training was communicated within the normal framework of a day-to-day intimate relationship between the disciple and his master, or teacher.

The Christian tradition under which most of us have been reared dictates a **pulpit-congrega-**

tion relationship. It is patently clear that Christ required a more intimate relationship, a deeper level of commitment. He showed no interest in a relationship that was merely technical or professional. Anyone who seriously studies the method by which Christ trained His apostles will be amply rewarded. I believe that in Jesus' use of discipleship one will discover not only a valid alternative to pastoral care, but a more biblical and efficient one as well.

The conception of the church as the united Christian community in the city. The only way we can put into practice the truth that Christ, through His redemptive work, united us with Himself, forming one body of all the redeemed, is to determine to recognize every other Christian as our brother or sister. We are all children of the same Father. Consequently, we must learn to live together. To do that, we must rid ourselves of all the sectarian barriers in our minds. It is no less than amazing to discover how effective sincere love of the brethren is in bringing down those barriers and overcoming the differences between us!

As pastors, we must humble ourselves and draw closer to our fellow-pastors of different denominations, in order to know each other, to help each other, and to pray together. We need also to be liberated from the strict confines of our buildings and religious programs, while multiplying the ministry and activities carried out in the homes. In a word, our common commission is to shine together as a single bright light in the city. In that way, those around us will see that Jesus Christ is truly Lord, because it will be evident in a community that shines with His light and truth.

We are persuaded that God Himself has determined this. He has given us His grace and His blessing. Christ said that all authority belongs to Him, in heaven and on earth The only proper response from a believing and obedient people is: Yes, Lord! Thy will be done!

Promisis